Edward Howard House

The Midnight Warning

And Other Stories

Edward Howard House

The Midnight Warning
And Other Stories

ISBN/EAN: 9783744670104

Printed in Europe, USA, Canada, Australia, Japan

Cover: Foto ©Thomas Meinert / pixelio.de

More available books at **www.hansebooks.com**

"'COME AND GIVE ME YOUR HAND, MY DEAR BOY'"

[Page 1

THE MIDNIGHT WARNING

and Other Stories. By
EDWARD H. HOUSE. With
Twenty Illustrations * *

NEW YORK
HARPER & BROTHERS, FRANKLIN SQUARE
1892

CONTENTS

ILLUSTRATIONS

THE MIDNIGHT WARNING

A Southern Tale of Fourth of July in War Time

I

It was on the afternoon of the Fourth of July, 1861, that my father resolved to throw away all reserve, and confide to me, his eldest son, the difficulties and dangers of his position, the purposes he had formed for immediate action, and the hopes which he cherished for the future.

I was in a state of such bewilderment that I could scarcely control my thoughts. Only a few hours before a strange and startling event had occurred, for which I was totally unprepared, and which had gone far to unsettle many of my boyish ideas of right and justice. It was not easy for me, at my age, to recover from a shock so suddenly and so unexpectedly received.

At eleven o'clock in the morning or thereabout, while I was working in my mother's

1

flower-garden beneath our parlor windows, my
attention had been attracted by the approach of
a body of horsemen rapidly advancing from the
eastward. I gave them only a casual glance,
having not the slightest anticipation that they
intended to favor us with a call. Visitors to our
house had not been numerous of late, although
there had been a time, not very remote, when
the planters of the neighborhood were never
tired of accepting and enjoying my father's hospitality. I had no suspicion that there were especial reasons for their gradual falling off, and
the disturbed condition of the district was sufficient, it seemed to me, to account for all social
irregularities; but I was soon to be more fully
enlightened, and in a way as humiliating as it
was alarming.

Instead of passing our gate, the cavalcade
turned in and rode swiftly to the front door,
which stood open at all seasons.

"Come in, gentlemen," my father called out,
cheerfully, from the porch. "Ptolemy will see
to your horses. Call the boys, Ptol; look
sharp."

The old negro was quickly at hand with a
number of assistants, and in a few minutes the
unlooked-for guests, of whom there were not less
than half a dozen, were seated in the parlor,

while their host was setting the usual refreshment on a table.

"Help yourselves, gentlemen," I heard him say, with his accustomed cordiality; but to my surprise the invitation met with no response. After a moment, the awkward silence was broken by a voice which I recognized as that of Judge Huntoon, a well-known resident of Helena, whose pride in his reputation as an orator of the most approved South-western pattern was a matter of common notoriety.

"We are here, Colonel Claiborne," he began, stiffly and pompously, "to perform an unpleasant office. Our fellow-citizens of Phillips County have delegated us to wait on you and express the general regret at your failure to co-operate in their measures for the welfare of our government and country."

"It is true, judge," my father replied, with characteristic gentleness, "that I have given no substantial proof of fidelity to my country in this unhappy crisis, but it is not lack of devotion that restrains me. You and most of my neighbors are aware that I am bound to my home by duties which I have no right to disregard."

"We fully appreciate the claims of your family," responded Judge Huntoon, gradually becoming grandiloquent, as was his fashion when addressing even a small audience. "You have, sir, our deepest sympathy in the afflictions which have befallen you. It is not required by your friends that you deprive those who are dearest to you of your companionship and care, but we justly demand that the moral support of so distinguished a citizen of Arkansas shall no longer be denied to us. You have had many opportunities, since the State proclaimed its emancipation from Northern bondage, of declaring your loyal adherence to the Confederacy. You have availed yourself of none of these, and your omission to do so has provoked criticism. We now call upon you to make open affirmation of your principles, as becomes a patriot and a worthy son of the South."

"You have chosen a singular day for an errand of this description," my father remarked, as calmly as before.

"We have chosen it deliberately. It seemed fitting that you should be accorded the privilege of announcing your allegiance on the chief anniversary of that nation to which we once belonged, but which we have been compelled to renounce and abjure."

"There can be no better occasion for avowing my allegiance—my undying allegiance," said my father, in a tone that singularly affected me.

"That ought to be sufficient, gentlemen," exclaimed Judge Huntoon. "I congratulate you, Colonel Claiborne, on the fortunate result of this interview. And now, I think, we may join in drinking prosperity to the righteous cause, and confusion to its enemies."

"I could do that with all my heart and soul," said my father; "but I feel that there should be a clearer understanding between us, and—"

"Right you are, sir," broke in a third party to the conversation, whom I knew by his peculiarly broad plantation accent to be Major Brindal, a prominent local politician and one of the fiercest advocates of secession. "The judge will excuse me if I say this matter needs a good deal more clearing up than it's likely to get by his delicate handling. What the people of Phillips County expect, Colonel Claiborne, is that you'll come out of your shell—clean out, once and for all. If you can't take the field, as most of us hope to do, you can at least put yourself square on the record, and let us know that you're a stanch friend of the new flag. There's been too much delay already. We want the truth, the whole truth, and nothing but the truth; and we want it now!"

"So far as I am concerned, Major Brindal, you shall have it," returned my father; "and I may

add that you, or others, could have had it at any
time during the past six months, if you had seen
fit to ask for it. My old friend the judge, like
all men of his standing, needs no assurance that
I yield nothing to your importunity which I
would not more readily have conceded to his
courtesy. It is not my habit to force others to
listen to my convictions, but that does not mean
that I have none, or that I desire to conceal
them. You have come here to satisfy yourself
and the community as to my loyalty and patriotism. Take away no doubt with you, gentlemen, concerning my sentiments. I would lay
down my life, I would forfeit everything but
honor, for the country into which I was born
thirty-nine years ago; by which I was trained
to manhood, on the banks of the Hudson River,
a score of years later; for which I fought in
Mexico, to the best of my strength, in forty-
eight; and under whose mild and tolerant government I have since dwelt in happiness and
peace until the outbreak of this causeless war-
fare. That country, you well know, is the United
States of America. I acknowledge no other,
and while Heaven permits me to draw the breath
of life none shall take its place in my affection,
and no power shall cause my faith and trust in
it to falter."

I was almost paralyzed with amazement, and, I will frankly admit, with terror as well, as I listened to these words. Up to that moment, I had not dreamed that my father's opinions were in any serious degree opposed to those of the majority—I may say the almost unanimous majority—of our section. I knew he had been a firm Union man in past years, but it never occurred to me that he would venture, or even desire, to dissociate himself from the great movement in which, I fancied, every Southern-born American was bound to take part. This seemed so much a matter of course that I had thought it wholly unnecessary to question him upon the subject; and his habitual repugnance to political discussion accounted, in a good measure, for the silence he had maintained in the early stages of the Rebellion.

Knowing the temper of the neighborhood, and the ungovernable fury which possessed many of the popular leaders, my first apprehension was for my father's personal safety. I leaped up to the window beneath which I had been standing, and climbed into the parlor, determined to hold myself ready for any emergency. In the excitement that prevailed, my entrance was unnoticed. The visitors had sprung to their feet, and were talking so violently that no one of them

could understand the other. All were gesticu-
lating wildly around the tranquil figure which
stood unmoved amid the clamor, in the centre of
the room.

"I told you how it would be, gentlemen,"
shouted Major Brindal, who was the first to gain
a hearing. "This crazy abolitionist will be letting his niggers loose upon us, if we give him the
chance."

"That is no part of my duty," said my father,
smiling faintly, as if amused at the major's bois-
terous demonstration. "The servants are in no
fit condition to receive their freedom. I wish
they were, for it will come to them only too
soon."

"Colonel Claiborne," the major screamed, "you
speak like a madman!"

"I speak without violence, sir, and without forgetting that there are sick and suffering wom-
en in the house. Unless you can moderate your
tone I shall hold no further parley with you."

"The colonel is right," said Judge Huntoon,
with ponderous formality. "This is not the
place for heated argument. But the exigencies
of the public service—"

"Allow me, judge," interrupted my father;
"now that you tell me I am an object of unfriendly scrutiny, I am entirely willing to meet

my fellow-citizens at any time—this evening, if you like, in Helena Court-house—and define my position in the clearest possible manner. That will probably be better than to continue what might become an angry disputation under my own roof."

"It seems to me, however," said the fire-eating major, "that proper precautions should be observed."

The sheriff of the county was one of the party of inquisition, and at this point he thought it proper to interfere.

"No precautions are necessary," he asserted. "I don't know what you mean, Major Brindal. The colonel's word is a sufficient guaranty for his appearance, and for the fulfilment of his promise. I fervently trust that in the interval he will convince himself of the expediency of modifying the dangerous doctrines he has imprudently avowed."

Five minutes later my father and I were left alone.

"Say nothing to your mother about this disagreeable scene," he warned me, "unless you are directly questioned. Leave me for an hour, Lionel, and then come to me in the library."

The caution was scarcely needed. I knew how important it was to keep my mother free from agitation. She had lain for months, hovering between life and death, the victim of a frightful steamboat disaster on the Mississippi. My grandmother had been terribly injured by the same explosion, and my grandfather and one of my sisters had been killed outright. Our home was filled with hopeless grief and anguish, for we had learned that neither mother nor grandmother could ever recover, though the fatal result might be long delayed.

II

At the appointed time I joined my father in what we called the library, but which was in fact rather a business office than a place for studious retirement. I saw at a glance that a change had been made in the disposition of its few familiar decorations. Over an engraved portrait of Washington, always the most conspicuous object in the room, was draped a silken flag of the Union, which had been given to my father by his young bride when he started southward with his regiment, in forty-eight, and ever since carefully preserved, though rarely exhibited, even to members of the household. A likeness of Jefferson Davis, under whose immediate command my

father had served in Mexico, which had long held
a prominent position, was now displaced and deposited on the floor, the face turned to the wall.
Upon a cushion, in a recess, the family Bible
had always rested, but I observed that another
book, of small size, which I did not remember,
had been laid beside it.

" You know, Lionel," said my father, "that I
have no fondness for meaningless shows. But I
wish to impress you, on this day of noble memo-
ries, with the sacredness of two objects, one of
which is the emblem of my political faith, and
the other the foundation of my political convictions. I fear that I have never made you comprehend what this flag means to me; and I
am sure I have too long neglected to guide
you to a proper understanding of the priceless
legacy left us by those who framed our government. I have been to blame, but from this time
forth it shall be my chief duty to repair the
fault."

"I had no suspicion that your feeling was so
strong, sir."

"I wished your boyhood to pass without the
anxieties which have beset me in recent years.
But I should have seen how impossible it is even
for the young to escape the evil influences of
these days. I trust no harm has come from my

delay. You have not allowed yourself to be misled by the follies of our neighbors?"

"I did not imagine that you were against them, sir. I thought you were perhaps indifferent; nothing more."

"If your mother did not need me every day and hour I should now be far away from this spot. Nothing but her grievous strait could keep me from offering my service where it is due."

"But, father, you cannot live in peace with the people hereabout after what you have said to-day."

"I could not live in peace with myself if I continued to conceal the truth. I am not sorry the occasion came. I looked for it sooner, for I gave good cause for distrust by refusing, last month, to join in the celebration of that wretched mêlée which our friends persist in calling the glorious triumph at Manassas. Since I have to take a stand in opposition to my old associates, there cannot be a better day than this for doing it."

"Will you really go to Helena Court-house, this evening, and defy them?"

"I shall go to declare my position, that is all."

"It will be the same thing to them. You will take me with you, father?"

"Not for the world. Think of your mother, if—"

He did not finish the sentence, nor was it necessary. I understood him well enough. I knew that he risked his life in venturing among the desperate men he had pledged himself to meet, not in fellowship, but as an enemy to the cause they worshipped. I knew, also, that nothing would turn him from a purpose to which he had set his mind, and that, although he might go to his death, he would go without shrinking. My heart was heavy as I listened to his instructions for my future conduct in the event of calamity to him. But I strove not to add to his tribulation by showing the dread which nearly overcame me, and before the afternoon was ended I had gathered from the example of his splendid spirit a courage of which I had never before been conscious. I felt, indeed, child as I was in years, that this Fourth of July must be the birthday of my own manhood.

He went to Helena, and returned in security. The respect he had earned by his upright and unselfish life, and the gratitude with which the citizens remembered the many public benefits he had conferred, were his safeguards at this moment of trial. But he had lost forever the affection, and probably the good opinion, of the community which had before been ever ready to exalt and do him honor. From that day

existence was made a weary burden to him.
He was regarded as an outcast, and condemned
to an isolation which was relieved by no single
sign of sympathy, even from those who had been
his deepest debtors. The malice, the contumely,
the insolent brutality with which he was per-
secuted would have crushed a man of less indom-
itable will; but no word of complaint fell from
his lips, and I recall no interruption to the
patient dignity which sustained him through
months of sorrow and privation.

The flag which my father loved was carefully
put away on the morning following the Fourth.
He did not wish to expose it to any chance of
insult or mockery, nor was he inclined to excite
animosity by openly displaying it. But the little
volume I had noticed, which was a copy of the
Constitution of the United States, and which now
appeared to command his reverence beyond all
books save that beside which he had placed it,
remained in constant use. It became the basis
of a course of study by which I was made acquainted with the principles in defence of which
he was willing to accept a life of sacrifice and
pain.

I shall not attempt to describe the miseries of
that cruel winter. My grandmother died before
the incoming of the year 1862, and early in the

ensuing summer my dear mother followed her. I well knew that after this event nothing would long detain my father. He waited only for the opportunity to break away from the galling inactivity to which he had been condemned, and he felt that this was near at hand when the news came that General Curtis, with a sufficient Union force, was about to establish himself on the western side of the Mississippi, fixing his headquarters at Helena.

On the Fourth of July, 1862, I was again called to our library to receive my father's final orders, previous to his departure. The silken flag had been taken from its hiding-place, and hung once more over the Washington portrait. The Constitution, which I now knew so well by heart that its covers were seldom opened, was in its place of distinction, near the Bible. My twin-sister Jennie, and my little brother Julius, nine years old, were also summoned to this interview.

"I made a mistake," my father said, "in keeping you, Lionel, so long ignorant of what it was needful you should learn. We must not let Julius grow up without a better understanding of our obligations to the only country that a Claiborne can honorably acknowledge. He is too young to grasp more than the simple outlines of the situation, but he knows why I must leave you,

and with what purpose I go. Instruct him in
the right course, so far as his years will allow,
and make him what a loyal American's son should
be, until I can take him under my own care again."

I promised, fervently and faithfully, for my
father's labor had borne good fruit, and he could
not have asked for a sincerer disciple of his national faith than I had become through his wise
and earnest teaching.

"And now, my boy," he continued, "from this
day I give over to you the charge of our home
and the guardianship of your sister and brother.
It is a trust which I know you will fulfil with
diligence, and you will not find it too heavy a
burden, for you have a steady head on your fif-
teen-year-old shoulders, and have thoroughly
learned the necessary lessons of prudence and
self-restraint. I can leave you only a little money, but the plantation will supply most of your
actual needs. Some of the negroes will stand by
you to the last extremity. I cannot answer for
all. I have given them to understand that they
are free, so far as my will can liberate them, and
that I believe they soon will be so declared by
the law of the land. Those who choose to remain under your control until peace is restored
will find me then ready to help in fitting them
for their new condition. Many, however, will

prefer to seek their fortune in their own way, and of course they cannot be stayed by you. I do not think that my fellow-citizens who have honored me so liberally with their disfavor will harass you after I have gone. The Southern people are not inhuman, no matter how misguided they may be, and the worst of them would take no pleasure in molesting a family of children haplessly deprived of their parent's protection. They will bitterly assail me for what they will call my desertion of you, but I can heed no reproach for obeying the commands of my conscience. Come nearer to me, my dear ones. Let me say farewell while we stand together beneath the flag for the sake of which I part from you, and under which, by God's blessing, we shall surely be reunited, in happiness and love."

He left us at nightfall, and, passing through the Union lines, was warmly welcomed as a worthy accession to the body of skilled soldiers then gathering around the great general who was presently to lead the armies of the nation, one after another, to the proudest victories of modern history.

The year went slowly by, with few events to vary the monotony which settled upon our household. Though we had little to cheer us, we were seldom called upon to endure actual hardships.

2

The people in the vicinity were not unkind, and
some among them were apparently ready to befriend us to a certain extent; but, remembering
the bitterness of their rancor towards my father,
I could not respond to any of their advances,
and we were gradually left to the solitude which
we preferred to any companionship that our locality could afford.

I worked hard at all seasons, assisted sturdily
by old Ptolemy and a dozen more of our best
servants, who never dreamed of abandoning the
homes in which they had been reared. But for
their lively humor the loneliness would have been
almost unbearable. We heard twice from father
during the winter, the letters being brought out
secretly by scouting parties. Frequent communications were impossible, for General Curtis
kept his troops, as a rule, well within their for-
tifications, and it had been clearly pointed out
by the neighbors that I should be sharply dealt
with if I attempted to wander from our premises towards the river.

With the spring of 1863 came indications of
active movements on both sides, and small bod-
ies of cavalry began to circulate through our
part of Arkansas, doing little damage to one another, but a great deal to the property of the
inhabitants, who were roused to an irritation

which manifested itself in many disagreeable
forms. By various acts of incivility we were
made aware that a new feeling of hostility was
growing up against us, and I had to exercise constant caution to avoid being drawn into ugly
quarrels. I should not have thought it desirable to acquaint father with these causes of dis-
comfort, even if I had been able to do so, but he
had means of knowing almost everything that
went on; and I received a message from him in
May, telling me that if he found we were likely
to be driven too hard, he would either get leave
of absence and come for us, or send a trusty messenger to extricate us from our position and take
us to him. But he did not wish to decide upon
our removal unless it became a matter of grave
necessity.

From this time onward I was in constant dis-
quiet. I should not have felt so ill at ease if I
had been alone, for I had no doubt that I could
make my way out of the disturbed region at any
moment; but I feared for those who looked to
me for preservation from peril—my young brother, and my high-spirited sister, who never could
reconcile herself to the restraints of our position.
Scarcely a day passed without the appearance of
Southern guerilla bands; and though I was dis-
inclined to believe that our neighbors would go

so far as to excite the animosity of these raiders against us, it was certain that some of their demonstrations, as they rode wildly by, were anything but pacific.

A little before sundown on the third of July, 1863, as I sat on our piazza, looking anxiously up and down the Clarendon Road, a single rider came in view, galloping at breakneck speed from the direction of Helena. He checked his course at the gateway, and I at once started down the avenue to meet him; but before I had half crossed the lawn he was flying onward again, and I lost sight of him as he entered a thicket about half a mile distant.

Ten minutes later he came tearing back more furiously than ever. I was now standing at the gate, and as soon as he caught sight of me he stopped short and began to examine me keenly.

"Are you Lionel Claiborne?" he inquired.

"That is my name," I replied.

"You answer the description. Tell me your father's full name."

"Andrew J. Claiborne," I promptly responded.

"Exactly; the 'J' stands for Jackson, of course—Andrew Jackson Claiborne."

This made me suspicious. My father's second name was not Jackson, as it happened.

"Why do you wish to know?" I demanded.

" Perhaps I've a letter for you if you are the right person," he answered, drawing a parcel from his coat-pocket.

"I can't say how much I thank you," exclaimed I. " We haven't heard from him since—"

" Since when ?"

" Since Clayton's raid, last May."

" Correct. And the ' J ' stands for—"

" Julius," said I, without hesitation, this time; for a glimpse of father's handwriting on the envelope had put an end to most of my doubts.

" One more question, my lad. I am a friend of Colonel Claiborne. If this is his house, there's a recess in the library which should hold two books. Tell me what they are, and I'll hand you the document."

" One is our family Bible—"

" And the other ?"

I looked at the stranger steadily, and believed that I saw honesty and good faith in his countenance. Nevertheless I could not all at once place myself entirely at the mercy of a man whom I saw for the first time.

" If you are my father's friend," I said, " and have heard from him about the contents of our library, you must know that I cannot speak of them to everybody."

" True enough ; I'll give you a start. To-mor-

row morning you will go through the ceremony
of hanging something above a big picture on the
wall.   There; if that doesn't satisfy you I'm
afraid you're hard to please."

"It does satisfy me.   The book you refer to is
the Constitution of the United States."

"Here you are," cried the horseman, tossing
me the letter.   "Read it carefully and act ac-
cordingly.   I can't stop to talk, for the whole
State of Arkansas is broke loose, and, by Hanky,
a good part of it is at my heels.   To-morrow—"

His sentence was cut short by the sharp crack
of a rifle, and he spurred away without another
word.   Then there came a rattling discharge
from the upper road, and a dozen bullets flew
past, one of which caught the escaping rider's
hat and sent it rolling in the dust.

As I was picking it up a small detachment of
cavalry surrounded me, and the leader hurriedly
began to inquire who it was that had scampered
off in so desperate a hurry.

"You gave him no time to tell," I answered,
pointing to the hole through the hat.

"Did he say nothing at all?" asked the officer.

"He said the whole State of Arkansas was
after him, and he had no time to talk."

"Struck it about right, he did;" and the cavalry leader laughed grimly. "Federal scout, I reckon. We'll wait here for orders, boys."

III

I SPEEDILY learned that a good-sized army under the Confederate general, Holmes, was close at hand, advancing to attack the Union troops at Helena without delay. Before midnight a number of regiments had marched by and taken position a short distance below our deserted gardens. By nine o'clock in the evening the lower part of the house was filled with Southern generals and their staffs, for whom I provided, with the assistance of my brother and sister, such refreshment as our limited store would allow.

They were all unknown to me, and it probably did not occur to them that any inhabitant of that red-hot section could be other than a stanch adherent of the Confederacy, though their confidence was so overweening that I doubt if anything would have made them feel the need of cautious speech. The only member of the party who appeared in the slightest degree uncertain as to the result of the forthcoming battle

was an elderly soldier, whom his associates addressed as General Price. The others were jubilant in the belief that they would sweep the
handful of Yankees into the Mississippi before
the following day was half over.

I was scarcely noticed as I went from room to
room, listening intently while the plan of the
proposed engagement was freely discussed and
the certainty of victory loudly proclaimed. My
heart sank when I calculated the strength of the
combined Southern force. From what I heard
on all sides, it could not be less than 10,000.
Early in the winter Helena had been occupied
by a powerful body, under Curtis and others, but
this had since been reduced to a single division,
led by General Prentiss. The remainder had
gone farther south, to take part in the operations
against Vicksburg. I knew nothing positive as
to the present number of the garrison, but had
reason to believe, from reports brought me by
our negroes, that it could not be more than one-
fourth of the attacking army.

Was the Union commander prepared for so
unequal a contest? Was he, indeed, prepared
for any contest at this time? Several of the
Southern officers seemed hopeful of carrying the
town by surprise, though General Price urged
them not to trust too blindly to that expectation.

Young and inexperienced as I was, I could understand that a great crisis was at hand, and that, apart from public considerations, my own poor little destiny, and that of my family, depended largely upon the events of the next twenty-four hours.

To what use could I put myself in this perilous emergency? I asked this question repeatedly, but found no answer. What could a boy of sixteen do, however willing and eager? What would my father have me do, if he were here? My father! I remembered suddenly, with a pang of self-reproach, that, in the whirl of confusion following the arrival of the soldiers, I had not given a second thought to the missive received some hours before. The absorbing incidents of the evening had driven it from my mind, and it lay unopened in the pocket where I had at first hastily concealed it.

I lost no time in seeking my own chamber and breaking the envelope. It contained only these few lines:

"MY DEAR SON,—On receipt of this you will put the house in order and make ready for departure, with Jennie and Julius, at the shortest notice. If fortune favors our cause, of which all of us who follow Grant are happily assured, you

will be summoned on or soon after the coming
Fourth of July. Meanwhile, I charge you to be
steadfast, and leave no duty to your country unfulfilled.   Your loving

"FATHER."

"No duty unfulfilled!" What *was* my duty?
Our household affairs needed no attention, for I
had so disposed them, weeks before, that we
could set forth without an hour's delay at the
cost of only a few trifling sacrifices. Since I
learned my father's wishes, in May, this had
been my chief concern, and the consciousness
that I had labored faithfully to execute his orders was the chief consolation of my dreary existence.

What duty now remained? I sat on my cot-
bed and pondered for nearly an hour, when a
flash of intelligence came into my mind. It was
now eleven o'clock. Quickly descending to the
lower floor I entered the parlor in which the
Confederate commanders were still holding coun-
cil. To a young officer who seemed less busily
engaged than his seniors I addressed myself
thus:

"Can you tell me, sir, if your lines are outside
of our grounds? I have to make my rounds before going to bed."

"You look too tired for any more work, my boy," he answered, kindly. "How far do you wish to go?"

"As far as both ends of the plantation. It will not take very long, but I don't want to be stopped on the way."

"If it is necessary—"

"I should feel that I was neglecting my proper tasks if I failed."

"Very well; you shall have a pass."

He went to the table and spoke to one of his superiors.

"Certainly, Captain Fairchild," was the reply. "Make out the permit, and I will sign it."

"Please call on my brother for anything you need," I said to Captain Fairchild, while he was writing. "He is a little fellow, but you'll find him bright for his age."

"Here is your pass;" and the captain handed me a bit of paper. Bending down, he whispered, "The word for the night is 'Pemberton.' Be careful how you use it."

"Thank you, sir," I replied. "I had better not disturb you when I come back. I will go straight to my room, unless I hear that you want me."

I ran to my sister's chamber, gave her a longer good-night kiss than usual, and told her to retire

as soon as possible and keep old Nurse Tilly
with her till the morning. To my brother Julius I said that I had to ride across our fields, and
might not return till very late; but he was not
to make the least remark upon my absence, and
must simply do what he was bade by our visitors, without entering into conversation upon
any subject.

In less than five minutes I was in the saddle,
and on the way to the north-eastern boundary
of our estate. I did not think it wise to cross
the patrol lines on the high-road, but determined
to follow the interior paths until I was well beyond the range of skirmishers. I had not a par-
ticle of difficulty in getting through. It amused
me, however, to observe that most of the sen-
tries, after examining my safe-conduct with elaborate scrutiny—turning it upsidedown, and even
staring at the back, where there was no writing
at all—allowed it to be evident that they could
not read, and insisted on having the password
into the bargain. Some of them mumbled that
it was too dark to see the written signature,
though the moon was shining with uncommon
brightness.

It was fortunate, therefore, that the good-natured captain had thought to provide me with
the double security. I wondered at the readi-

ness with which the privilege of free egress had
been accorded, especially on the eve of a battle;
but, as I have remarked, the Southerners were
too triumphantly confident of success to be governed by ordinary discretion. Still, I was sure
that if any of the party occupying our house
had known me, or if a single neighbor had been
present to tell the story of my father's fidelity
to the Union, I might as well have asked for the
command of General Holmes's army as for the
slightest civility from one of its leaders.

I must admit that I was not wholly satisfied
with the manner in which I was repaying Captain Fairchild's generous trust. That consideration gave a very uneasy turn to my reflections.
But my father had never suffered me to doubt
that the demands of the country were first of all
entitled to obedience, or to believe that obligations of patriotism could be honorably evaded,
no matter how strongly they might conflict with
our selfish instincts of pride and vanity. I was
sure of his approval, and I remember that it appeared to my overwrought imagination, in that
hour of enthusiasm, that his letter, so opportunely delivered, had really come to me as a direct
token of admonition and encouragement.

As I had hoped, the outer picket line of the
Southerners was within the limits of our own

property. Having passed it at a secluded and unexposed spot, I kept on in a north-easterly direction for perhaps ten minutes, and then turned southward, striking the high-road at a distance of about ten miles from Helena. Thenceforward I was at liberty to make up for wasted time. It was but half an hour after midnight when my gallant little mustang brought me in view of the heavy earthworks that guarded the town. Forgetting the requirements of prudence, I was rushing onward at a headlong rate when a shout from the wayside arrested me.

"Halt! Who goes there?"

"A friend! a friend!" I cried, nervously, pulling my pony to his haunches.

"Come on, friend, if you have the word," responded the sentinel.

"I haven't the word, but I bring important news—very important."

"Wait there," exclaimed the soldier, harshly, coming out from shelter. "Get away from under that tree into the light."

I did as I was commanded, and he moved slowly forward, narrowly watching me at every step.

"Who are you?" he asked, when he reached my side.

"A friend of the Union," I replied. "I live

eleven miles out, on the Clarendon Road. Let me go to General Prentiss."

The guard laughed softly.

"We'll see about that," he said, and began to question me on various topics.

"You are taking a great risk," I warned him. "Money can't measure the value of what I have to tell your general."

He seemed impressed by this, and by my earnestness, and led me with great caution to a guard station not far away. The sergeant in charge was quicker than his subordinate to appreciate the situation, and I was immediately blindfolded and taken, still on horseback, by a winding course, to a spot which I guessed to be in the centre of the fortification. Here I was ordered to dismount, and the bandage was removed from my eyes.

IV

SEATED at a table in the open air, before a large tent, was a person of evident rank, whom I had once or twice seen passing our place, attended by a small escort of cavalry. Several aides stood by him.

"What have you to say, young man?" inquired this officer, who wore no distinguishing uniform.

"I am speaking to General Prentiss, I presume," were my first words.

"Never mind that," he answered, curtly. "What brings you here?"

"I beg your pardon, general; I asked because I have a great deal of information, and there may not be time to tell it twice over."

"I will take care of that," he returned. "Be quick with your story."

I then repeated, as concisely as I could, what I had heard respecting the plan of Holmes's assault upon the town. For a time the Union general listened indifferently, but when I began to state the particulars he showed more interest, and directed one of his officers to take notes of my report.

"Go over that again," he said, at one point. "You tell me that you had these details from General Holmes's own lips."

"Every word, sir; either from him or those next him in authority."

"They attack at daylight?"

"At daylight. Price begins the battle by storming the outer central works on the Cemetery Road."

"Did you hear what his force is?"

"General Parsons has a brigade of 2000. He marches upon the front. McRae, with about 1500, will try to get at the rear."

"Go on."

"An infantry body of 2000, under General Fagan, will try to carry a redoubt at your left— Fort Hindman, they called it ; and Marmaduke, who also has about 2000, will strike the fort on Reiter's Hill—your right, I heard them say."

"How is that? Marmaduke has nothing but cavalry."

"Yes sir, so I understood. They are to be dismounted for this fight. So is Walker's brigade, a thousand strong. They will make for an earthwork to your north, on the road to Stirling."

"You didn't mention that before," broke in a stout, swarthy officer, jumping up from a camp-stool and stepping towards me.

"I was just going to, sir, when the general asked me to begin again."

"The river works are all right," said the gentleman whom I took to be General Prentiss to the stout speaker. "The *Tyler* alone can take care of them. Now, boy," he added, turning to me, "what about the artillery?"

"I didn't hear much about it, sir. I am sure they have artillery, but I think—"

"Well?"

3

" My opinion goes for very little, sir."

" Let us have it, all the same."

" It struck me that they did not mean to rely much on their artillery. They are dead sure you cannot stand against their foot-soldiers. They say they outnumber you four to one."

" They are mightily mistaken, then," exclaimed the general, abruptly, and giving me a keen glance. "What strength do they claim altogether ?"

" Close upon 10,000, I judge."

" And all ready to clean us out at sunrise, and cook us and eat us for breakfast, hey ?"

" They are very confident, all except General Price. He wasn't so hot for the engagement. He said there was no chance of a surprise."

" Did he send you to tell us that ?" said the general, rising suddenly, and peering into my eyes.

I felt that my face showed red as fire by the light of the lantern which he caught up and held before me.

" I have nothing more to say, sir," I answered, with as much composure as I could command, though I could not keep my voice from trembling. " I came on an honest errand. I see it has been a failure."

" We shall know better about that to-morrow.

Orderly, look after this young man for the night.
Make him comfortable—and keep him close."

"But I can't stop, sir," I said, in alarm. "I
must go back at once."

"Oh no; we have no desire to lose your company. Simmons, here, will take care of you for
the present; till after to-morrow, we will say."

He spoke ironically, perhaps with the purpose
of irritating me and throwing me off my guard;
but, though bitterly mortified and angry at his
implied suspicion, I controlled my feelings for
the sake of those at home.

"I beg you, general, to consider my position,"
I cried. "I have ridden eleven miles at midnight, and hazarded more than my own safety,
to bring you this news, because I believed it to be
my duty. I have left my young sister and brother
alone, surrounded by Southern troops. Do you
wish to reward me by exposing them to danger?"

"What do you mean by danger?" he answered,
impatiently. "The Southern troops are not
likely to injure a boy and girl of their own
soil."

"Don't say that, sir. They have no idea whose
house they are in, but if any informer should
breathe a word of my father's record, his children's chance would be a hard one. I *must* be
there to protect them."

"I'm afraid you are trying to play too clever a game, young man. Who is your father?"

"Colonel Andrew Claiborne. He is serving with General Grant."

The officer was already moving away, but as he caught the name he stopped short, and I noticed that all of those who were grouped around the table rose from their seats and drew near me.

"Dan Claiborne? Incredible! I never heard that any part of his family stayed behind in Arkansas."

"We have been living at home, three of us, since he entered your service, last July."

"How could he leave you in so frightful a situation?"

"He *had* to go; he couldn't stand it any longer. During the first year of the war, my mother— but you don't care for this, sir."

"Indeed I do, my lad. I care for anything that concerns Colonel Claiborne and those who bear his name. Speak freely."

"My mother was so ill that he was bound not to forsake her. It was a dreadful life the people made him lead, for I believe he was the only loyal man in the whole county; but he held on till after her death, and then went away, leaving me in charge of everything. He couldn't take us with him, and yet he couldn't stay."

"And how have you fared?"

"Not so very badly, sir. I have had to keep myself mighty quiet, and of course all our old friends had given us up from the beginning. But it might have been worse. You won't stop me now, general?"

"Bless my soul, no; not if you wish to go. Yet—wait a moment, and don't take offence at what I am obliged to do. Orderly, find the messenger who brought the despatches from Vicksburg, two days ago. Bring him immediately. He asked permission, yesterday afternoon," continued the general to his companions, "to ride out on the Clarendon Road and reconnoitre. Let us see what it was all about."

In less than a minute, it seemed, I saw before me the man who had delivered my father's letter on the previous evening. His face brightened with a smile of recognition.

"You appear to know this youngster," the general said.

"It's Colonel Claiborne's son, by Hanky!" replied the new-comer. "I'm right glad to meet him again. I have a message for him from his father."

"That is sufficient. I beg your pardon, my young friend, for doubting you a little bit, and I thank you heartily for the good turn you have done us. Gentlemen," he remarked to his officers, "the report we have heard takes a very definite value now. You will oblige me, Mr. Claiborne, by clearing up one or two details, and then you are free to do what you deem best."

I had never been called "Mr. Claiborne" in my life, and it amuses me to remember that I was enough of a child to be as absurdly elated by this trivial puff of distinction as I was gratified by the general's assurance of confidence. After holding me in conversation about a quarter of an hour longer, he bade me good-night, expressing an earnest hope that before the week was over he should be able to welcome me to his quarters under circumstances widely different from those of this unceremonious flying interview.

The messenger from Mississippi asked and obtained leave to accompany me a part of the way as I rode homeward. He had much to tell me about my father and the position of trust and honor to which he had risen in the Union service, and some wholesome counsel to give for my present guidance.

"These wild Western rebs are a heap too brash," he said, just before turning back to camp. "Old Holmes is going to get an awful licking to-morrow, in spite of the big crowd he has at his back. I wish you were out of these diggings, my boy.

The Johnnies are like a pack of wild animals,
after a defeat, and if they had the least concep-
tion of what you've been up to—well, you know
all about that; it's no use talking over ugly possibilities. Take good care of yourself. If ever
you needed prudence you need it now, as sure as
my name is Jake Rumford. Your father has it
in his mind to come up for you, as soon as Grant
scoops in Vicksburg, and that's only a question
of days. But this is going to be a scary region
for young folks of your training, with a runaway
secesh army howling and rioting over the land.
My advice to you, if you're not under positive
orders to stay, is to seize the first chance and get
over to Helena with your brother and sister.
Your work this night gives you a claim that our
people can't overlook, and the general will be
glad to see you safe down the river to Colonel
Claiborne. Think it over; think hard. You've
given yourself a start that ought to open a career
for you. Don't spoil the opportunity. Let your
father have something to rejoice at, not to grieve
over."

The good-hearted scout shook me warmly by
the hand, and I made the quickest possible time
between the outlying pickets of the opposing
forces.

V

On nearing our plantation I took care to choose a different place for crossing the lines from that at which I had passed out. The guards looked sharply at me, but did not question my right to be admitted, nor delay me longer than was necessary to spell out the permit. I went through the fields, far beyond the mansion, making a wide circuit in order to approach the gateway from the upper road. When I rode through it, at four o'clock, Holmes's troops were already stirring. Dismounting in the stable-yard, I hunted up old Ptolemy, and, cautioning him to say nothing about my long ramble, sent him to call my brother out to me. From Julius I learned that Jennie and he had gone through the night without disturbance in their part of the house, although the occupants of the lower story had been rather more lively than was agreeable. After giving him some necessary instructions, and sending word to Jennie that she had better keep to her chamber until I could speak with her, I proceeded, without going in-doors, to busy myself in the open air.

Captain Fairchild was the first of our military lodgers to make his appearance. He greeted me pleasantly, remarking that I looked as if I had not slept, and asking if it had been a hard night for me.

"You see, sir," I answered, evasively and with a good deal of awkwardness—for it went against me to deceive so kindly a man—"we never before had so many soldiers about the house, and it falls on me to look after everything."

"Well," he said, "you can take plenty of rest after we go. You won't be disturbed again. We shall sleep in Helena to-night, and for some time to come."

"Then I suppose you call it a dead certainty —to-day's fight."

"You may reckon on that," he replied, laughing gayly. "This will be Prentiss's second surrender, unless he runs faster than he did at Pittsburg Landing, and gets aboard of a gunboat before we can catch him."

"I'll say good-bye, then, captain; probably this is the last time I shall see you."

"Oh, I hope not," he said, quickly; "I would like to ride out for a call, now and then, if—if it will not be displeasing to your sister."

I looked at him in surprise. What in the

world had my sister to do with the coming or
staying away of this young officer?

"I took the liberty, while you were absent,"
he added, "of sending her a message by your
brother. Some of our people were a little noisy
in the night, and I wanted her to know that she
should not suffer the slightest personal inconvenience, no matter how much patriotic hilarity
there might be about the house. I considered
that this was due to the young lady whose hospitality we had rather abruptly demanded."

This puzzled me more and more. To hear
Jennie called a young lady, and spoken of as if
she were the head of the establishment, was even
more odd than to be myself addressed as Mr.
Claiborne by an officer in the opposing army.
She was sixteen, to be sure, and well grown;
but, after all, she was only a girl.

"It was very good of you, sir," I said, thinking that these military gentlemen on both sides
had exceedingly polite manners when they chose
to be agreeable.

"Not at all, not at all. I noticed, early in the
evening, that she was a lady of very—very superior intelligence, and—and great charm of manner. I was much concerned for her comfort. I
wanted her to know she was entirely safe."

I stared at him so hard that he probably sup-

posed I was too stupid to comprehend him; for
he went on, in a very elaborate and precise style,
to state that it was because he feared his freedom
might have offended her that he desired to pay
his respects, at some future day, and make his
excuses.

"Why, how could she be offended by an act
of courtesy?" I asked, bluntly.

"You think not? Well, I trust you are right.
I should be sorry—I wonder if—I mean that it
would gratify me extremely if I could be permitted to take leave of her before I go; but I
suppose that is out of the question, at such an
hour."

"Dear me!" I exclaimed; "if that is all, I'll
call her at once—or perhaps you had better come
with me." I felt that I owed him something,
after all that had occurred, and would have
gone a good deal out of my way to please him;
but what possessed him to make a point of taking leave of Jennie at four o'clock in the morning, I could not imagine. He had bidden me
good-bye, which any one would think ought to
have been enough.

However, Jennie came readily out of her room,
looking a trifle feverish, I regretted to observe,
and listened quite properly, with her eyes cast
down, while Captain Fairchild spoke to her in

so low a tone that I did not catch a word.
"Good gracious!" I thought to myself, "how
fast she is growing up! It never struck me before." She bowed, just like a little woman instead of a child, and the captain uncovered his
head to her as deferentially and with as much
ceremony as if she were a queen and he were on
dress parade; though in fact he had no idea as
to who she was, and probably had not even heard
her name. They didn't talk long, but she must
have said something nice and clever—Jennie had
the knack of making pretty speeches—for he
laughed softly when he left her, and kept on
smiling all the way down-stairs and across the
lawn.

As soon as he had finally gone, I hurried back
and urged my sister to get to bed and nurse herself. She was quite flushed, and her eyes were
dancing so flightily that I recommended a dose
of quinine to quiet her nerves. She tossed her
head and said something that sounded like "Ri-
diculous-I-never-how-can-you-Lionel!"—running
the words all together without a break anywhere, and winding up her incoherent remark
with a hysterical giggle that made me more
anxious than ever. I asked if the commotion
and worry had not been too much for her, but
she declared she liked it, and insisted on hearing

everything that Captain Fairchild had said about her. I told her how he had called her a young lady, and all that, and begged to know if she could make anything out of it.

"Lionel," she answered, "if you should try to count the geese we have on the place, you never could get the number right. You would be perfectly sure to leave out one—and the biggest of the flock."

I don't repeat that as an example of Jennie's pretty sayings. She did not favor me with these as often as she did other people; perhaps she thought they would be wasted on a brother. But she was a fine girl, for all that, and one to be proud of, as I shall very soon show.

Before five o'clock the house and grounds were all clear of strangers, and the army was winding its way towards the river. We sat down to breakfast, and I gave an account of my midnight adventures, to which Jennie, who had fortunately recovered her steadiness without taking either repose or medicine, listened attentively and thoughtfully, while Julius was thrown into such excitement that he could scarcely swallow his food.

"I am glad you did it," said my sister. "You could not have forgiven yourself if you had let the chance go by. I know what father will think. But there is one thing that grieves me."

"What is that, Jennie?"

"It is a pity you had to deceive the only gentleman who took pains to treat us handsomely. I wish it had been some one else."

"That hurts me, too," I replied; "but there was no other way."

"I shall not dare to look him in the face again," pursued my sister.

"You will hardly have occasion to," I said, wishing to relieve her; but she did not seem grateful for this attempt at consolation, and reminded me that Fairchild had distinctly announced his intention of coming to see us.

"Why, Jennie, he thinks the Northerners are going to be beaten. I don't believe any such thing. And if Holmes is driven back, we may not remain here a week longer, you know."

Not long after this we heard the sound of cannon booming at a distance. The attack had begun. Heavy clouds of smoke rose in the east, and we watched them with anxious minds and grave faces until near nine o'clock, when we bethought us of the duty belonging to the day. For the first time, we were separated from father on a Fourth of July, but we knew what would

be done if he were here, and what he would wish
us to do in his absence.

We went to the library, which had seldom
been used during the past year, and our hearts
were filled with tender recollections of the dear
parent who had constrained himself to leave us
only because his conscience told him he would
be a coward if he stayed. I placed the worn
copy of the Constitution where he had laid it
on the two preceding anniversaries, and Jennie
brought in the old flag. We did not immediately hang it, however, being interrupted by Ptolemy, who came shuffling through the hall to an-
nounce that a great crowd was in sight on the
lower road, half hidden by the dust it raised, but
evidently coming towards us with a swiftness
which he could not understand.

"They are running away," I cried, exultantly.
"Thank Heaven, they are whipped!"

It was a hasty conclusion, but it turned out to
be correct. The assault had failed at every
point. The best fighting on the Southern side,
we subsequently learned, had been done by
Price, the one general who had doubted the
wisdom of giving battle. The others had con-
tributed no effective support, and by nine o'clock
the entire army was in retreat.

We ran to the front of the house, and were

soon able to distinguish the mass of fugitives
swarming in our direction, without order or
method, defiant of discipline, more like a mob
of maniacs than a body of reasoning beings. I
ordered the negroes to keep themselves carefully
hidden, and, after closing all the doors, hurried
up-stairs with Jennie and Julius to the garret,
from a window of which we watched the frantic
throng as it whirled by.

VI

THE horror of that scene passes description. I
have heard, and I believe, that it is only under
the strain of a blind and senseless panic that humanity becomes utterly degraded, casts away all
its noblest attributes, and sinks to the level of
the brute creation. The rabble that writhed and
fought and raved in mad endeavors to elude a
purely imaginary pursuer was composed mainly
of brave men, yet no quality of manliness, far
less of courage, was visible in the frenzy of its
furious flight. The sole impulse was to escape
at any cost, reckless of decency and insensible to
shame, from an absurdly fictitious danger; and
to compass this end, the most hideous and re-

volting excesses were resorted to. In their delirium of terror these half-crazed beings, united an hour before, by ties of friendship and by devotion to a cause which they held sacred, were guilty of atrocities which would have shamed wild beasts.

For half an hour the disgraceful rout continued, until the greater part of the army had gone by. Their groundless fears had protected us thus far from intrusion, and we rejoiced to believe that we were now free from molestation. We did not know that there may often be more mischief in a single straggler than in a host of scared and swift-footed runaways.

We descended to the lower floor, Jennie going straight to the library, while I went forth, taking Julius with me, to find the servants and set them at work. As I entered the house again, I was startled by a succession of heavy knocks at the front door. Bidding my brother keep silence, I ran around to the piazza, where I found a tall, gaunt man, evidently a cavalry private of the retreating force, hammering with the butt end of a pistol against the panels. He glared at me fiercely, and cried out:

"Open the door here! What do you mean by keeping people out at a time like this?"

"Are you wounded?" I asked.

4

"Wounded—no. Hungry and thirsty—yes. And tired. Open, or I'll burst in, double quick."

"No need of that," I said, quietly; and I called to Julius to take down the fastenings, which he promptly did.

"Whar's your whiskey?" was the fellow's first demand, as he strode into the hall, his long sabre clashing noisily after him.

"I have no whiskey to give you," I replied. "You can have some coffee if your people have left any, and something to eat."

"None of that!" he shouted. "Bring along the whiskey, or I'll soon find it."

"I've told you there is none for you."

He let loose a blast of wild words, and started to explore the premises. After looking into the parlor and discovering nothing to his fancy, he pushed on towards the library.

"Don't go there!" I exclaimed; "that room is private."

"Aye, that's whar the liquor is," he retorted, flinging open the door and disclosing a scene the sight of which sent a chill of dismay through me.

My sister stood at the top of a step-ladder, festooning our cherished flag around the picture-frame. She uttered a faint cry, and sprang to the floor. The trooper cast his eyes savagely around for what he was in search of, and did not

at once recognize the Stars and Stripes hanging
overhead. Presently, however, he glanced upward, and with a yell of rage pointed to the detested banner.

"Ho, that's the game, is it? Making ready
for the Yanks! Git up thar, gal, and haul it
down. Sharp's the word!"

My sister looked at me without stirring or uttering a sound.

"Down with it, I tell ye, or I'll set the house
afire."

"Pay no attention to him, Jennie," I said.
"Take Julius away and leave him to me."

"Not a step," he roared, as he cocked his big
six-shooter and flourished it threateningly, "Pull
down that rag and fetch it to me."

"Do you come here to show fight to a girl
after running away from Union men?" I sneered
—very foolishly, no doubt, as I had no weapon
and was wholly in his power.

"I fight with people who fly that flag—men,
women, and children; and I mostly kill 'em
when I can. You stay whar you are, gal. This
young bantam shall do the job. Now," he called
out furiously to me, "fetch it here, unless you
want a bullet through your skull!"

He looked and spoke as if he were in dead
earnest, and Julius, who had till now stood

dumb with fright, made a spring towards the hall.

"I'll get the boys in," he gasped, breathlessly.

"Hold up, young 'un. Thar's a bullet for you, too, if you budge another inch."

"What shall I do, Lionel?" cried my little brother.

"Do nothing, Jule; let this man deal with me."

"Jes' so; I'll deal with ye. Up ye go, before I count three, or I'll scatter your brains over the carpet!"

He pointed the revolver straight at my head. Jennie made a movement as if she would rush between him and me, but I put up my hand to check her. She was as white as a corpse, and her whole body shook so that she could scarcely stand.

"Shall I—shall I take it down?" she stammered.

"Never think of such a thing," I replied, with all the energy I could command. "Remember who first hung it there."

"Forgive me, Lionel; it was for you I asked."

A torrent of imprecations burst from the ruffian's lips. "Take your last chance," he screamed. "Now—*One!*"

Julius began to sob piteously, and my sister caught at the desk to save herself from falling.

" *Two!!*"

"Tell father, Jennie—" I could say no more, for a lump seemed to rise in my throat and choke me. I bent my head, and waited.

"*Three!!!*"

A crash and a blinding flame followed, but I felt no hurt. A shriek from Jennie made me look first at her. She was gazing with dilated eyes upon the assassin, and I, turning about, saw with infinite relief that he was struggling in the clutch of a man taller and more powerfully built than himself. It was Captain Fairchild, who had entered almost at the instant the shot was fired, barely in time to strike the pistol aside and save me from a horrible death.

The soldier, though active and sinewy, was no match for his new antagonist, who speedily wrenched the weapon from his hand, and with a blow in the chest sent him staggering across the room.

"What is the meaning of this outrage?" said Fairchild. His features were quivering with wrath.

"I didn't see your uniform, captain," answered the desperado. "Took ye for another of these pison varmints."

"How dare you draw your pistol in a private dwelling?"

"Private dwelling! You'll find it's a nest of white-livered traitors. Jest lift your eyes to that thar wall."

The captain looked, and his face darkened.

"This is a surprise to me," he said, with obvious displeasure. "But it is not a matter for a subordinate to pass upon. Who made you judge —and executioner?"

"You see, cap, it kind o' riled me to think of them critters spreadin' out that pesky banner to curry favor with the Yanks jest after they've got the best of us, for once. I ordered the boy to haul it down, and he refused. I've got no marcy for a boy like that."

"Do you know anything else to his discredit?"

"No," drawled the soldier; "can't say I do— not to be sure of. Seems to me I've seen him somewhar before, but I don't exactly fix him. Better let me take him in hand, cap."

"Certainly not, sir. I shall do what is necessary."

"Guess I must have a finger in it," persisted the fellow, insolently. "I reckon I'm not under your orders, anyway; and I've set my mind on giving this wriggling sarpent what he desarves."

"Stand back, you scoundrel, or I'll teach you what discipline is, with your own weapon. As for you, young man, I thought better of you than this. It's a poor business to turn renegade when your friends are in misfortune, and to bid for your enemy's grace with false flatteries."

At this unjust imputation Jennie sprang valiantly forward.

"Captain Fairchild," she exclaimed, "I will not hear you accuse my brother so unfairly, so ungenerously. You spoke of discipline a moment ago. Well, sir, we believe in discipline. There is only one authority that this household is bound to respect. We have *not* waited till the day of your defeat. Lionel is under orders to unfold the Union flag every Fourth of July, as it always has been unfolded; and I would not *own* him if he disobeyed!"

"I should be glad to accept your statement, miss, but I know of no authority that can override the laws of the Southern Confederacy."

"Then I can tell you, sir, that my father's children are governed by his instructions alone."

"Indeed," said the captain, apparently undecided whether to smile or to be vexed at her impetuosity. "May I ask who your father is? You forget that I have not the honor to know your name."

"He is Colonel Andrew Claiborne."

Fairchild started back as if he had been

struck. "Claiborne, the Unionist!" he cried. "Are you telling me the truth?"

"It is my habit, sir," answered Jennie, loftily.

"Yes, yes; pardon me, but this is a shock. Who could have foreseen such an extraordinary circumstance?"

"Hold hard, captain," broke in the lawless cavalryman, who had been eying me viciously for some minutes. "I have spotted this 'yar young reptyle at last. I can locate him now. He went down through our lines towards Helena last night, while I was on picket. I let him go by, myself. He had the word and a written pass."

The captain's look of reproach and scorn stung me beyond endurance. "And I gave them to him," I heard him mutter, with something that sounded like a groan.

"We're in a trap!" the trooper howled. "It's as plain as daylight. We are surrounded by a gang of spies, and this house is their headquarters. Look alive, cap. Follow my lead, and get out of this like lightning."

VII

He darted away before he had finished speaking, but Fairchild gave no heed to the warning or the invitation. He remained motionless for a short space, fixing his eyes alternately upon Jennie and me. At last he spoke, and what he said cut like a knife.

"It seems, young man, that you rewarded my indulgence by a base betrayal of trust. It may be that we owe this horrible disaster to my imprudence and your deception. I don't doubt that I should be justified in taking your life, but I spare you because the punishment would partly fall on one—on those who cling to you with affection; and I do not lift my hand against women and children. To you, Miss Claiborne, I will say that though your presence protects your brother from the consequences of his crime, I am no longer under an illusion as regards yourself. The esteem of an honest man cannot be given to a girl who I know is the sister of a spy, and who, since she does not blush for his infamy, is perhaps herself a—"

"Don't speak that word," I broke in, before he

could end his sentence; "not to her. You'll regret it as long as you live. if you do. Call me
whatever you like, but don't put any vile name
on my sister."

"I am glad to be anything that Lionel is," said
my brave Jennie; "and what he has done I
would do, with all my heart and soul!"

The dear girl tried to be firm, but the strain was
too much for her, and in the very effort to hold
herself erect and defiant before the young officer,
she tottered and would have fallen to the ground
if he had not leaped forward and caught her,
fainting, in his arms. A single look at her insensible face wrought a great change in him.
There was not a trace of his haughty disdain left,
as he turned appealingly to me.

"I am a cowardly brute!" he cried. "What
shall I do?"

"She must be taken to her room," I said.
"Julius, come and help me."

"Let me, let me," pleaded the captain. "Stay,
I am stronger than both of you together. I will
carry her alone."

Without waiting for an answer he lifted her
as easily as if she had been an infant, and was
half-way up the staircase before I had clearly
taken in his purpose.

He remembered where to go, and when I

reached Jennie's chamber he had already deposited her in an arm-chair, and was regarding her with painful solicitude.

"If I have hurt her," he murmured, "I have hurt myself a thousand times worse."

As if to reassure him, Jennie opened her eyes and surveyed us.

"It is nothing," she whispered; "only my foolish weakness."

The captain would have had more to say if he had not been interrupted by a loud bustle below. Footsteps were heard through the passages, doors were opened and shut violently, and a confused clamor of voices announced the arrival of a considerable party.

VIII

WHO could they be, these new and perhaps dangerous visitors? As we listened in anxious suspense, a cry rose distinctly above the tumult.

"Claiborne, Claiborne! Are you anywhere in hearing?"

The sound of my name reassured me. "Here am I!" I shouted, without reflecting that the summons might come from an enemy and not from a friend. But the immediate response showed that my instinct had not led me astray.

"Come on, boys, he's safe, thank the Lord;" and we heard a scuffle upon the staircase.

"Don't let any one come here," exclaimed Jennie; "not for the world!"

I saw my error and sprang to obey her, but it was too late. A crowd of Union soldiers poured into the room, headed by Rumford, the scout, who set up a cheer of delight on seeing me.

"Hurrah, boys; all's well now. I've been scared to death about you, my lad. Thought the beggars had snaked you off with them. It's a comfort to set eyes on you. And, by hanky, you've got a prisoner, too!"

"No, no," I protested; "nothing of the kind. This is—"

"This is a rebel captain," said Rumford; "and nothing else but a prisoner."

I did not dare to look at Jennie, for I saw that Fairchild had straightened himself up as stiff as a ramrod, and put on the same hard and contemptuous expression that his face had worn a few minutes before in the library.

"Do I understand," he inquired, addressing Rumford in a tone of rasping sarcasm, "that I owe my capture to this young—Southern—*gentleman?*"

"That's about the size of it," replied the scout, with cheerful alacrity.

"It isn't true," I declared, indignantly. "I have no hand in it at all."

"Well, we'll allow you the credit of it, any-how," said Rumford. "I want to make this Fourth o' July a big day for you, Claiborne."

"You'll make it a day of misery—"

"For the rebs," chuckled Rumford. "We've done that pretty well, already."

"But this officer—"

"Pray say no more, Mr. Claiborne," said Fair-child, peremptorily and very coldly. "I accept the fortune of war, even when the game is un-fairly played against me. I am a prisoner, as your friend states, no matter by what trickery I am caught. I am at his disposal. All I ask is that he will get me out of this house as quickly as possible."

I heard Jennie moan plaintively, but this time Captain Fairchild gave no sign of relenting, and seemed unconscious that she was near him.

"I don't know that we are bound to consult your wishes," said Rumford. "We expect to re-main here overnight, if young Claiborne will take us in, and you will have to stay likewise. To-morrow we'll rattle you back to Helena in short order. We want you to go, too, Claiborne

—you and your folks. That's what I'm here for. General Prentiss strongly advises it. He sent me with a squad of horse to keep mischief away from you till you were safe inside his lines."

"I don't know," I answered; "I can't say. My sister is all worn out by the agitation of last night and this morning. She may not be well enough to move."

"If she's sick, the more reason why she should get out of this ranch. Beg pardon, miss, for not saluting you before. No offence, I hope; in these hot times we often seem to be rude when our inclinations are all the other way. Upon my word, you ought not to tarry here twenty-four hours longer. If you're not strong enough to ride, we'll rig up a litter, and the boys that you select to carry you down to the river will thank their stars for the privilege."

"Let us talk about it by - and - by," I said. "Just now we will leave her to get over her fatigue."

"Of course. Beg pardon again, miss, for plunging in here so unceremoniously, but I was in a fever to get on your brother's trail. Come, boys, we're in the way here. As for this prop and pillar of the Confed, we'll have to put him under guard. Or perhaps we can make it easier for you, captain, if you give us your parole not to slip away."

"I ask no favors, sir," replied Fairchild.

"Just as you please. Call it a favor to us, if you like. You can make it more comfortable for everybody, all round."

"What is it that you wish?"

"I propose that you give us your word, as an officer and a gentleman, that you will not try to escape. Then we'll show you every consideration we possibly can."

The captain pondered, and looked here and there, undecidedly. I caught his eye, and contrived to signify, by a rapid shake of my head, that I was emphatically opposed to the suggestion. He appeared surprised, but after hesitating a moment longer, announced that he was not prepared to make the required pledge.

"I cannot afford to throw away a chance," he said. "No one knows what will happen. Our troops may rally and renew the attack. There may be a dozen parties, larger than yours, within rifle-shot of us. So long as I see a possibility of rescue, I will not bind myself."

Rumford almost cackled with derision. "There isn't an organized body a dozen strong between this and Clarendon," he declared. "Every man-jack of your army, except a few like yourself, is

on the dead run for the middle of the State.
They are the fastest Arkansas travellers on record.   But you shall suit yourself.   You only put
us to a little extra inconvenience, and I needn't
remind you what the penalty will be if you make
the least attempt to cut loose."

The captain bowed, and it was arranged that
he should be lodged in one of the rooms on the
second story, and a guard stationed at the door
with orders to treat him civilly if he kept quiet,
but to shoot him at the first sign of intention to
break away.   I suggested my father's chamber,
saying that it was now unoccupied, and could be
used as a place of confinement without incom-
moding anybody.   I had, however, another and
a very different reason for making this proposal,
which I shall shortly take pleasure in explaining.

This matter having been disposed of, I went
below with Rumford, who told me that several
officers, including possibly the general in command, were making ready to start down the Mississippi as soon as news should be received of the
fall of Vicksburg, which was hourly expected.
Transportation was offered to me and mine, and
it was hoped that we would make our preparations rapidly and report ourselves in Helena on
the morning of the fifth.

" You ought to be there now," added the jo-

vial scout, "celebrating the Fourth with the boys
in blue. I suppose you have forgotten there is
such a day, out in this benighted wilderness."

"Do you think so?" I inquired. "Come with
me, if you please."

I led him to the library, where the flag still
hung over Washington's picture.

"We can't do much," I said, pointing to it;
"but you see we haven't forgotten."

"By hanky, I should say so! I call this
plucky, with a drove of secesh savages tearing
and rampaging past your door. Lucky none of
them caught you at it."

"Why do you always call them savages?" I
demanded, having an uneasy impression that his
abuse was rather too persistent and indiscriminate.

"I don't, always. But it takes mighty little
to send a badly whipped army stark mad. I've
seen proof of it more than once, and on both
sides. Our own troops were like a pack of hye-
nas after the first Bull Run. There's nothing
to choose between North and South, in a panic.
You may thank your stars that the Johnnies
were in too much of a hurry to give you a call
when they went by. You'd have been in an ugly
fix, I can tell you."

It did not suit my purpose to inform him that

we *had* been in "an ugly fix," nor how opportunely we were befriended. After offering him and his comrades the refreshment I had refused to the rebel straggler, I went to Jennie, to consult with her about leaving home. But I found her full of another subject.

"Oh, Lionel, what will he think of us?" was her first wail.

"Who, the scout?"

"The scout!" she echoed, curling her lips contemptuously. "I detest him."

"Why, he's as good a soul as ever was," I said, very much astonished at this demonstration. "He came on purpose to help us."

"He has degraded us forever. Captain Fairchild believes we laid a snare for him — you and I."

"No, Jennie, he can't suppose that; or, if he does, he won't think so long."

"What do you mean—how can you prevent it?"

"Nothing easier; you'll see, by-and-by."

"Tell me at once. He saved your life, Lionel; think of him now, a prisoner in this house!"

"You leave me alone, Jennie. Am I the sort of fellow to let a debt like that go unpaid? Don't you ask too many questions, little girl."

But Jennie's bright, even temper seemed to

have deserted her on this occasion. She surprised me more than ever by bursting into tears —a thing I had not known her to do in our hardest times of trial. I tried to comfort her, but as I could not guess the cause of her grief, my efforts had no satisfactory result.

"Don't let this stain rest upon us," she sobbed. "To be called a—a *spy*, and by such a man as he is!"

"It makes no difference what any man calls us, so long as we have nothing to reproach ourselves for. Captain Fairchild will change his tune before to-morrow morning."

"Lionel, you shouldn't speak of him in that tone. Have you no sense of gratitude?"

"Jennie, dear, I can't understand you. Something strange has come over you. But you sha'n't quarrel with me; I'll run away, sooner."

And so I did. Later in the day I returned, however, and persuaded her to make ready for our departure on the following morning. Then I set to work upon a more difficult task, for the successful performance of which I felt that unusual tact and ingenuity were required—more, perhaps, than I could command.

IX

Taking a note-book and a pencil in my hands, and displaying them somewhat conspicuously, I went to the chamber in which Fairchild was detained. To the sentinel at the door I said:

"I don't want to disturb your prisoner, but I have to make a hasty inventory before we go."

"All right," replied the soldier. "He's quiet enough; you'll have no trouble with him."

I knocked at the door and waited for a response.

"Walk right in," said the guard. "Make yourself at home in your own house."

I followed his suggestion, and closed the door carefully behind me. The captain gave no greeting, but rose from the chair in which he was seated and stared freezingly at me.

"Will you allow me a few words, Captain Fairchild, in private?" I began.

"You have no need to ask, sir. My permission counts for nothing," he replied, as stiff and frigid as an iceberg.

It was necessary, I perceived, to approach him very delicately, if I hoped to gain a hearing.

"I appeal to your generosity, sir," I said. "Will you do me a favor?"

"I am not in a position to confer favors, Mr. Claiborne."

"You can do all that I desire, if you will only listen to me without prejudice. I ask it not only on my own account; it concerns my sister, as well."

"I am at your service," he answered, a red flush rising in his cheeks.

"I must be so brief," I proceeded, "that I shall trust you to fill many gaps that I may leave. Captain Fairchild, I am the son of a man whose whole life has been devoted to the service of the United States. He has suffered much for his fidelity, and has taught his children that they must expect to suffer likewise. While he lived here he allowed no Fourth of July to go by without calling us to witness his reverence for the flag of the Union. Now that he has left us, I try to follow his example. The flag was hung this morning where he used to hang it, without a thought of any good—or any harm—it might bring us. This much I think you can readily understand, and credit."

"I accept your statement, sir, thus far."

"My father has never ceased to instruct me that my country's claim was always to be first

considered. Only last evening I received a letter
from him, charging me to be steadfast and to
leave no duty unfulfilled. I had heard your
generals boasting of the ease with which their
overwhelming force would overcome the little
Northern garrison at Helena. I believed that
the cause which my father loves was threatened
with a great danger; and like a gleam of light
the thought came to me that I could give a use-
ful warning. You know what I did. With his
bidding fresh in my mind I could not act otherwise. I cannot say whether the news I carried
to the Union general was valuable or worthless.
At first he took it as if it were of no importance;
afterwards he listened with a good deal of care."

"It was of the highest importance," said the
Captain, despairingly; "and he had it through
my gross negligence. I deserve to be court-
martialed. I would demand a trial if I were at
liberty."

"I think you are in error. You gave me the
pass, it is true, but I could have obtained it from
some other officer just as well. If not, I should
have found a way to get through without much
difficulty. Well, sir, you have seen fit to call me
a spy. That has a hard sound to a Southern
gentleman's son. I know very little about military matters, but I have understood that a spy

was one who went secretly into an enemy's camp
to get information by any and every means—to
steal it if no other way would serve. I did not
do that. Your plans were freely talked of without an attempt at concealment, and I reported
them as well as I could. But I don't mean to
say that I would not have done a good deal more.
As I felt last night, and as I feel now, I would go
to almost any length to carry out my father's
command. If I have to be called a spy for it,
that can't be helped. I shall not consider myself humiliated unless he condemns me. I ought
also to make it plain that the ride to Helena was
wholly my own affair. Neither my sister nor
my brother had the slightest hint of my purpose."

"She said she would have done the same!" the
captain exclaimed.

"Yes, I believe she would, if the task had fallen
to her. But, as it happens, she was in complete
ignorance until this morning. And there was
one thing which none of us could have foreseen:
even if your army was to be defeated, we did
not dream that any of the Northerners would
come so quickly, or so far, as this. All through
it has wounded me, and my sister, too, to think
that a person who was kind and courteous to us
had been misled. Jennie grieved deeply about
it at a time when we had no expectation of ever

seeing you again. I ask you to put yourself in
our place, and consider what we must have felt
when we saw that you suspected us of setting a
trap for you and scheming for your capture.
Captain Fairchild, I would rather have been
shot by that cavalryman than be supposed capable of such shameful treachery."

I lost control of my voice just here, and stopped
abruptly. Presently the captain, in a milder
tone than before, told me to " go on."

" I will go on when I hear you say that you
believe me."

" I—I do believe you. I am glad to believe
you. Give me your hand, Mr. Claiborne. I
have been unjust; but at my age—I am not so
very much older than you, my lad — and under
such a trial as this disgraceful repulse, a man's
judgment may get all unhinged. I have wronged
you—and your sister."

" You have, a little; but the account will
be square if you do me the favor I came to
ask." `

" If there is anything I can honorably do—"

" No question about that. I was afraid you
would give your parole when Rumford proposed
it, and in that event it would have been inconvenient. Now you have simply to wait quietly
till night comes, and then let me have the satis-

faction of seeing you off in safety, and saying good-bye like a friend."

It was now the captain's turn to experience a slight difficulty in speaking; but he soon recovered himself, and said:

"Are you entirely in earnest, Mr. Claiborne?"

"Never more in earnest in my life."

"What will be the consequences to you?"

"We haven't time to discuss them. They can't be very serious, anyway."

"I am not sure of that. I must not take advantage of your youth and inexperience."

"It's your only way to prove that you no longer misjudge us."

"If that is the case, I— Would your sister say the same?"

"Certainly she would. Jennie and I are twins. I know everything that passes in her mind."

I am now aware that this was very far from the truth; but I said it in perfect good faith, and I really believe the statement would have been fairly correct twenty-four hours before. Strange things had happened to us since the previous evening. I had grown to be a tolerable makeshift for a man, and Jennie—if Jennie had not absolutely blossomed into a full-grown woman, she was so far on the way as to have put aside the transparent frankness of girlhood and begun the cultivation of secrets all by herself, without assistance from her brother.

"I should like to be convinced that you are right," said Fairchild, dubiously. "Will you take a line from me to Miss Claiborne?"

"Oh yes, if you wish;" but I thought it a flagrant squandering of time, nevertheless, and wondered that a practical man should fret himself about insignificant trifles.

He took my note-book and pencil, and scribbled to an extent that spoke ill, I inferred, for his faculty of concise expression. Being reminded that we might be interrupted, he ceased suddenly, tore out half a dozen pages, and handed them to me with the announcement that his course of action would be determined by the answer he should receive.

As I had no doubt what this would be, I proceeded without delay to prepare my plans, and hurried to the servants' quarters in search of Ptolemy, intrusting the note to Julius's care as I went out, and telling him to deliver it privately to Jennie.

The old negro was sitting in the doorway of his cabin, meditating over the recent stirring events, and looking forty times as wise as any judge that ever sat in our circuit.

"I want you to brush up all your smartness,

Ptol," I said. "I have something very important for you to do."

"Sholy, Mars' Liny, sholy," he replied, with immense gravity.

"I suppose you know there is a prisoner in the house."

"Mighty glad to hear it, Mars' Liny."

"Well, wait a minute. This gentleman is a friend of mine and Miss Jennie's. He ought not to be a prisoner."

"Co'se not; stands to reason."

"He mustn't come to any harm here, Ptol."

"Dat he sha'n't; nobody ain't goin' to trouble a hair on his head."

"Keep still and hear me. We must get him off the plantation this night."

"I'll 'tend to it, Mars' Liny."

"Can you really, Ptol?" I was taken aback by this prompt acquiescence, and feared the old man had been dazed by the occurrences of the past twenty-four hours and did not comprehend what I was talking about.

"Easy as winkin', Mars' Liny. Whar is he now?"

"In father's room."

"Firs' rate. You let him out de side do', an' I'll put him whar nobody can't find him."

"But how will you manage it?"

" Don' I tole you I'll 'tend to it?" said Ptolemy, with unspeakable dignity. "You jes' leave him to me."

"See here, Ptol; this is not a thing to joke about. It's a matter of life and death. This gentleman must get clear without a scratch."

"Hain't made a joke for fifty year, old Ptol hain't. Bress your soul, honey, don' I see you're all of a fidget? Ease your mind, chile; I'll git your frien' out safe an' sound. 'Tain't de fust time."

"I don't understand what you mean, but I tell you it would be a disgrace to us all if I failed to set him free. Why, I owe him my life, Ptol."

"Say no mo', Mars' Liny. I'd give mine, an' welcome, to pay him for dat. But it's as easy — you don' know how easy 'tis. If I don' run him clean off de plantation to-night, I hide him whar no white man can follow, till de coast's clar."

"It sounds almost too good to be true."

"Sho! Don' you mind when Major Brindal's boy Walter done run away? Nobody never found *him.* We kep' him snug, not five minutes' walk from here, till de time come—"

"Go ahead, Ptol."

"Tole you by-'m-by about dat, Mars' Liny. You trust me. Your fader wouldn't neber make old Ptol gib his word twice ober."

"I *will* trust you, and be grateful for your help."

"Dat's right, honey. What time you want me at de side do'?"

"At midnight, unless I send word otherwise by Julius. Do you care to hear anything more about this gentleman?"

"No, sar. If he's your frien' and Miss Jennie's frien', an' if he stood to keep danger from my old marster's son, dat's 'nough for me. Hab no fear; no trouble sha'n't go near him, true as I live and breave. I wouldn't *say* so if I couldn't *do* so."

I was much better satisfied with his manner than I had been at the beginning of the interview, but in fact I need not have given myself the least anxiety at any moment. The old man, like many of his class whose defensive instincts have been sharpened by dire necessity, was as cunning and crafty as a fox; and like most of his race when their affection has been gained by kindness, was true as steel to those he served. But he felt himself a personage of consequence in the household, and as my father had always humored his pretensions he was not disposed to tolerate any diminution of his importance at the hands of a youngster like myself.

It was now desirable to report progress to

Jennie, whose gracious humor I hoped to restore completely by the news I had to impart. I found my sister in her room, seated at a table on which a dozen or more freshly written sheets were scattered, to which she was adding with industrious rapidity.

"Ah, Jennie, drawing up a detailed account of transactions for father? Good girl."

"No, not exactly," she answered, less blithely than usual, it seemed. "Captain Fairchild has asked me for my opinion on certain matters, and I—"

"Good gracious! There's no occasion to deluge the man. Better let me carry him a message."

"I don't think that would do, Lionel. He seems undecided as to how he ought to act, and under the circumstances I can't refuse to give my advice."

"Oh, I say! My sixteen-year-old sister advising a man old enough to be her father, and an officer in the Southern army."

"Sixteen! You know better, sir. Seventeen next month. And he isn't old enough to be my— He's only twenty-three."

"How on earth did you learn that?"

"He—he says so—in his letter."

"Upon my word, young woman, this is a

precious state of things. What have you to do
with the man's age?"

"Don't be unkind, Lionel, after behaving so
splendidly—making it all up with the captain,
and offering to get him away. Think of what
he did for you, and—and he hasn't any parents
—and he's dreadfully sensitive about his conscience—he fears it will make trouble for me—
for us—if you assist him to escape—and it would
almost kill me to have him dragged off to prison
from our house—so how can you be so heartless,
Lionel?"

"Why, I haven't said a thing," I protested, in
amazement. But though I had been, I admit,
pretty stupid thus far, I could hardly fail to be
enlightened by the rosy streaks that now came
and went on my sister's face; by her tearful eyes,
and by the eager impetuosity of her speech. I
did not much like the look of it, but there was
no time for remonstrance or dissuasion, and so
far as I could hastily judge, the best course was
to send Fairchild out of reach as quickly as
possible.

"Lionel, I want to convince him that he *ought*
to go."

"So do I, Jen; we're of the same mind there.
Give me your treatise on the whole duty of a
young Confederate captain, twenty-three years

of age, and an orphan in captivity with a trouble-some conscience."

" I never knew you to be downright unfeeling before!" she exclaimed, reproachfully. " It isn't like you a bit."

" Don't worry, child; it's all right. Give me the brief epistle, if you like that better."

" It—I haven't—it isn't finished yet," she murmured, her cheeks getting ruddier than ever.

" Mercy sake! Are you going to make a serial of it? He'll never be able to wade through that ocean of literature between now and midnight."

" I *must* add one word more—only one. Sit down a minute, dear."

" Look here, Jennie; I don't know much about girls—that is, girls who are going to be seventeen next month—but I know enough to guess what their 'one word' means at the end of a letter. It's generally a word of about 10,000 syllables. So I won't sit down, if you'll excuse me. It will be better, after all, if I don't see Fairchild until late in the evening. I'll leave you to put in that word at your leisure—mind you spell it right—and I'll come with a valise for your mail after supper."

" You are a monster, and the plague of my life!" she cried, with as fierce an accent as she could put on. Then she came at me and kissed me an inconvenient number of times, and wound up by making a defiant face at me as I shook myself free and skipped out of the room.

X

At eleven o'clock, having seen Ptolemy in the interval and settled all preliminaries, I again presented myself at the door of my father's room.

"Prisoner asleep?" I asked the sentry.

"Guess not; heard him tramping around a while ago."

"I'll have to go in, anyway," said I; and a moment later I was alone with the captain, who appeared more impatient to get the reply from Jennie than to listen to my scheme for his liberation.

"The foolish girl has covered a ream of paper to say what might have been told in two words," I remarked.

He looked as if he wanted to resent my presumption in criticising my own sister, but made no verbal comment, and straightway devoted himself to the bulky missive which I delivered over.

6

"If you try to take in all that you'll lose your chance," I warned him. "She's determined that you shall go; that's the main point."

"Yes, I see that," he answered; "and yet—"

"There's no 'yet' in the question, captain. Jennie vows that she wishes never to set eyes on you hereafter if you refuse to follow our counsel."

She had not vowed anything of the sort; but I had found a way to overrule his obstinacy, and proposed to take full advantage of the discovery.

"Then I suppose I must consent," he said.

"Precisely; and now you will be good enough to let me direct things. Put up your letter, and oblige me by lying down on the bed with your face to the wall."

"Since I conclude to yield, I may as well yield without reservation," he said, stretching himself out as I desired.

I gathered together a few of father's effects which I really needed to carry away with me, and then opened the door softly and called the guard.

"Can you give me a lift with a trunk?" I asked. "Come in gently; if your man is tired, let him have a rest."

I pointed to the reclining figure, and the soldier silently nodded assent. Leading him to a closet, I went through the form of getting out a big portmanteau with his aid.

"Anything else?" he inquired.

"Nothing more, thank you."

"How long are you going to stay here?" he continued, dropping his tone to a whisper.

"Half an hour or so."

"It's dry work mounting guard in this dismal hall. Could you keep your eye on him while I go below and freshen up? I won't be long."

"Go, by all means. Take your own time. Likely as not he won't know you've left your post."

"Good enough; take my revolver?"

"No; better lock the door until you come back. Or, wait: I'll lock it on the inside and pocket the key. When I hear you tap outside, I'll open. Don't hurry; everything will be safe here."

He started off in high good-humor, and I, delighted at this unlooked-for piece of luck, made the door fast, and told the captain to jump up and get to work.

"Pull off that uniform as fast as you can," I said, "and get into this suit of my father's clothes."

"What for?"

"Don't ask; you'll see soon enough."

"I don't like this, Claiborne."

"Bless us, we can't go over the whole argument again. Jennie will be wild if she hears that you disputed her arrangement."

"Oh, if it's *her* arrangement—" That was all he said, but he became quite humble and docile, and proceeded to array himself in a shooting-jacket and corduroy trousers several sizes too large for him. While he did this, I stuffed his uniform with various loose garments which I rolled up for the purpose, and, placing it on the bed, moulded it into a pretty close and accurate resemblance to the human form. In the dimly-lighted room the imitation was sufficiently good to convey the impression that the captain was still lying there, sound asleep.

Fairchild smiled as he inspected my handiwork, but not very cheerfully.

"I don't like it," he repeated, shaking his head.

"It doesn't matter whether you like it or not," I said, with intentional snappishness. "Jennie likes it, and that's enough."

"True," he assented, submissively; and he offered no further objection.

I then explained my reason for having proposed that he be lodged in this particular room, which was that my father had long ago caused a rough staircase to be built for his private use, leading from a large closet, or dark anteroom, to the garden at the rear of the dwelling. This was to enable him to go in and out at early or late hours without arousing others of the family by passing through the house.

"That fellow's thirst was a godsend to us," I said. "Wait you here, captain, while I run down and see if the coast is clear."

Ptolemy was lounging about the side door, according to agreement. I gave notice that in less than five minutes our guest would join him, and delivered this final charge:

"Remember, Ptol, you have not only his safety, but our honor, in your care."

"Make your mind easy, Mars' Liny," he replied. "Your frien' shall be five mile away by to-morrow mornin', if he likes. Dere's nothin' in de world I wouldn't do to please you, and dis— why dis is easier'n go a-fishin'. Ask me to do somefin' hard, if you want to make Old Ptol happy."

"It is enough, Ptol. Do this job well, and I'll never forget it. Nor will Jennie."

Returning to Fairchild, I explained that he must now put himself under the old negro's lead.

"I would gladly go with you," I told him, "and see you off the plantation, if it were not too great a risk. I must be on hand here, you understand, to ward off suspicion. Ptolemy knows the byways hereabout better than I do—or anybody else; and he has secret avenues of his own, through which nobody can track him."

"Who is Ptolemy?"

"One of our oldest servants. There's not a man on the plantation more intelligent; and not a dog more devoted and faithful."

"Then good-bye, Claiborne. Take my farewell to your sister, and my grateful regards. Tell her that her letter will be a solace to me, and that I shall claim the privilege of answering it, even if I have to wait long for the opportunity. Tell her—"

"If I tell her how you kept on talking idly when you ought to have been half-way across the fields, she'll think it's your senses you meant to take leave of, not her."

I was rough, perhaps, but there was positively no way to manage him except by holding up Jennie as an object of terror, and threatening him with her displeasure. The idea that a fellow of his size and training could be scared out of his wits by the fear of a girl's frown struck me as the most delicious absurdity I had ever heard of. I'm older now. It's a good many years since I left off laughing at Fairchild.

He grasped my hand, and, saying not another

word, went down into the darkness of the night. I resumed my labors, and in about a quarter of an hour heard the guard returning through the hallway.   He rapped lightly, and I unclosed the door, indicating by a gesture that I did not care to talk, and leading him to suppose that the prisoner was fast asleep.

A little later, just before midnight, I looked in upon Jennie, and satisfied a part of her curiosity with respect to the captain's escape, which I regarded as having been accomplished beyond all doubt.   I say "a part of her curiosity," because if I had answered all her questions she would have tied me to the subject till sunrise.   She was sensible enough when I shifted her around to reasonable topics, and, chatting comfortably together, we "saw out" the most exciting and momentous day of our lives—the never-to-be-forgotten Fourth of July of 1863.

XI

I slept quietly after the long course of fatigue I had gone through until the following dawn, when an exceedingly turbulent dream took possession of me.   I imagined that our house was

surrounded by batteries of artillery, and that a
tremendous cannonade had been opened upon it
from all sides.   At the same time a mass of as-
sailants burst in through doors and windows,
filling the interior with a din of clashing arms
and fierce outcries. I opened my eyes and shook
myself, but the illusion was not immediately dispelled.   An extraordinary clatter was certainly
going on all over the place.   In the midst of it
my door was thrown open, and Rumford appeared in a state of high exasperation.

"That rebel jackanapes has given us the slip!"
he cried. "Get up, Claiborne, and see if you can
put us on his scent."

While I rose and dressed he told me that the
sentinel had kept good watch during the night,
and found nothing to make him uneasy.   Every fifteen minutes or so he had looked into the
room where the prisoner was confined, and believed that he saw him always in the same position on the bed; but when the early sunlight
came through the windows he noticed something unnatural about the figure, and on examination discovered it to be a "dummy."   But the
method of escape could not be conjectured.   In
spite of the heat, the windows had been bolted,
and they still remained fastened.   In any case,
they were too high from the ground to tempt

even a desperate man to jump from them. The only doors, except that which gave admission from the hall, opened into dark closets. A thorough search had been ordered, and my assistance was needed, first to furnish a minute description of the premises, and next to point out the spots in which a fugitive might be likely to conceal himself.

On going below, I found the whole party of visitors in the utmost confusion. Jennie was walking about unconcernedly, now and then exchanging a word with the servants, all of whom had been summoned to supply information. Her manner went far to relieve me from apprehension, and a glance at old Ptolemy's face satisfied me that he had done his work effectively.

The small side door under father's windows was soon detected, and Rumford inquired with what part of the house it communicated. I told him, without hesitation or reserve.

"Why didn't you remember the private passage when the prisoner was taken to that room?" he demanded.

I made no answer.

"Now I think of it," he continued, "it was you who suggested quartering him there."

I was still silent.

"Mr. Claiborne," exclaimed the scout, exploding suddenly, "do you know anything about this business?"

I had, from the first, intended to acknowledge my share in the transaction, and as I felt confident that Fairchild was in safety, I saw no reason for delaying the avowal.

"I know *all* about it," I announced.

"Then it was *you* who outwitted us and set him free!" cried Rumford, while his companions in arms gave vent to their indignation by angry murmurs.

"There's no occasion to make a disturbance," I said. "I don't propose to deny what I have done. Captain Fairchild is out of your reach, that's certain. I shall tell the whole story to your commanding general, and take the consequences, whatever they may be."

"Mighty fine talk! It's a toss-up whether we ever see the general again. Ten to one your rebel runaway will gather together a lot of his riffraff and try to cut us off. He knows how few we are, and can find plenty to join him in a raid for revenge."

"He's not that sort of man. I'll answer for him."

"Your guarantee don't satisfy me, young man."

"Take mine, then!" exclaimed Jennie, coming

forward heroically and confronting the scout. "I *know* that Captain Fairchild is incapable of a mean or unmanly action."

I declare I was not the least astonished of those who witnessed the little girl's valorous demonstration. "Little girl" do I say? She seemed to look down on every one around her, though most of the army boys were strapping fellows. And how handsome she was, while the fire blazed in her eyes and the blood reddened her cheeks! Jennie was getting altogether beyond me; there could be no question about that.

Rumford gazed at her with a little amusement and a good deal of admiration.

"Oho!" he chuckled, grinning all over his weather-beaten countenance; "*that's* how the land lies." And, simple as the remark was, it sent my poor sister's magnificent bravery flying, and wilted her down in an instant from a creature of majestic stature and spirit to the ordinary level of her sex. Just for a second, indeed, she had rather the aspect of a timorous child than of anything more exalted.

But the scout was as good-hearted a fellow as ever breathed, and would not have wounded her sensitiveness for the world. Pretending not to notice her discomfiture, he said:

"Very good, miss; it's all right. I'll accept

your guarantee. I didn't know he was an old friend of yours."

Hereupon Jennie blushed more than ever, and I had to sniggle by myself at the notion of an " old friend " whom we had never seen or heard of thirty-six hours before. Rumford kept quite a solemn face, however, and said he was very glad to learn that the young Southerner was one of the right sort and a man to be depended upon.

" But, for all that, we may as well get started the first thing after breakfast," he remarked. " Our communications with headquarters are a little irregular, and the sooner we are there the better."

Before leaving, Jennie and I had to go through a sad scene with the servants. Ptolemy had guessed that the separation was coming, and controlled himself tolerably well. But his wife, Aunt Tilly, broke down completely at parting from the children whom she had nursed in their infancy, and whom she loved with all the tenderness of her simple and kindly nature. It was hastily decided that our little following of negroes, a dozen altogether, should remain on the estate under Ptolemy's leadership, and care for themselves until we could resume possession. If, however, the temper of the neighborhood should render that impossible, they were to go in a body to the camp at Helena, where—so Rumford assured us—they would be properly cared for. and given the means of earning their livelihood.

We left our home in sorrow and dejection, scarcely daring to hope that we should ever see it again, notwithstanding the confident expectation we had held out to the negroes. But we were sustained and cheered by the prospect of being reunited to our father. I could not believe that this happiness would be denied to any of us. It was impossible to doubt that I should suffer punishment, and probably a severe one, for my complicity in Fairchild's flight. but at least I should have the privilege of a parent's support and protection in the trial that awaited me.

On arriving at Helena I at once solicited an interview with the general in command, but was informed that he was too busy rejoicing over the great news from Vicksburg to give immediate consideration to my insignificant affairs. The great news was the surrender of Pemberton, which had taken place almost simultaneously with the defeat of Holmes, on the morning of the Fourth. The meeting I asked for was deferred till evening, and I then found that the general had already been informed of what had occurred at my home.

"Rumford has given me an outline," he said; " but if you wish to be more explicit I will listen to you."

I told him everything, making no effort to put myself in too favorable a light, and declaring my readiness to accept whatever penalty might be awarded. But I expressed a very earnest desire that this should not be of a kind to prevent our family from coming together again.

" You recognize that you were guilty of a serious offence," said the general, in a way which puzzled me extremely.

" I do, sir."

" Of course you would not think of repeating it, under any circumstances ?"

To this I made no reply. How could I? Jennie, who sat by my side, gave me what she intended as a comforting squeeze of the hand.

" I am afraid," he went on, " that this is too heavy a matter for me to pass judgment upon. I must shift the responsibility to a higher authority. General Grant will know better than I what to do. There's no appeal from him. I shall send you down the river to-morrow. Perhaps I shall go at the same time; if not, one of my aids will take charge of your case. Wait a moment; I'll find out exactly when the boat will start."

He retired to an adjoining room, and we heard him talking in a low tone. Suddenly a great burst of laughter broke out, as if the whole staff were enjoying a particularly fine joke.

"Barbarous wretch!" whispered Jennie. "All the time he was talking to us I felt that he was making sport of our misfortunes."

"I thought so too," said I; "but we will bear it as patiently as we can."

The general returned, and announced that we must be ready for the journey at nine o'clock the next morning.

"Can you tell me, sir," inquired Jennie, tremulously, "what my brother will have to undergo for his fault?"

"Really, I cannot. I shall have nothing to say about it."

"I thought, perhaps," she continued, "it might be something which I could share, and make it lighter for him. I am just as much to blame as he."

"My dear child!" began the general, with a vehemence that made me start; but he checked himself, and added, more calmly — "I'm afraid our code makes no provision for young ladies who connive at the evasion of rebel officers. You're not in a position to say you knew nothing about it, are you?"

"I could never say that, sir," said Jennie, turning very pale.

"You might perhaps acknowledge that you are sorry for it," the general suggested.

"Sorry!" she cried, her voice ringing like a bell, although the tears were now streaming down her cheeks; "I should be a coward and an ingrate to say I was sorry. I never was so happy as when I knew he was safe!"

"There, there," he rejoined, with what I took to be a clumsy attempt to soothe her, "I mustn't plague you any more. Your Captain Fairchild is a lucky fellow. Truly he is. I hope he deserves his good-fortune. Dry your eyes, my dear, and keep them bright till—till the war ends. It sha'n't last forever, I promise you. Keep a good heart—for somebody."

He took her hand in one of his, and patted it with the other. Then, saying that business was pressing, he wished us good-night and withdrew.

"Never mind him, Jennie," I whispered. "The old bear doesn't know any better. He is a barbarian, as you say."

I thought she needed sympathy, and wanted to give her a little. This is what I got for my pains from that utterly incomprehensible sister of mine:

"How *can* you, Lionel? You don't understand him at all. He is the dearest old gentleman that ever wore a uniform!"

XII

OF the meeting with my dear father at Vicksburg, two days later, I must not try to speak. The hardships we had gone through were all forgotten. What cared we for past perils and privations in the joy of finding ourselves once more under the loving care of the best and noblest of parents? The happy hours flew by so swiftly that the evening came before we had told him one-half of what had befallen us during the long term of separation; and we had scarcely approached the subject which we felt was the gravest and the most difficult of all when a messenger appeared, bringing a request that Colonel Claiborne would report himself, with his family, at headquarters. Then we saw how wrong we had been in neglecting to explain our position at the outset. Father expressed some surprise at the summons, but instantly prepared to obey it. We had little doubt as to why we were called, and, as we made our way through the disordered

7

streets of the recently beleaguered city, I hastily related what I had done, and what I expected the outcome would be.

"I should have heard this before," said father. "What prompted you to set the officer free?"

"I prompted him, father!" exclaimed Jennie. "He had just saved Lionel from being murdered."

"My dear, there is no sentiment in war. Your brother's act will be condemned, I fear, without consideration of his motive."

"Is General Grant so very severe?" asked Jennie.

"He is stern, though always just. But he is not likely to trouble himself about this matter— that is, unless I can persuade him to interfere."

"Why," said I, "the general at Helena declared it must be settled by the highest authority. He particularly told us that General Grant alone could decide the case, and sent me here for that purpose."

"I can't imagine what he was thinking of. He knows, of course, that a commanding general pays no attention to such trifles. Perhaps there is something behind it all, of which you are still ignorant. But we shall soon learn. Let us hope for the best. General Grant *can* interfere, if he chooses to. I have never asked a favor yet, and I don't think I should be refused the first time.

But I must make myself sure that I am justified in asking it. even for you, my son."

We entered the house occupied by the general-in-chief, and after a slight delay were shown into a room where several officers and a few gentlemen in plain dress were seated. Near one of the former was a lad about thirteen years of age, who showed a lively interest in the younger members of our party, gazing at us, I thought, with a very amiable expression. The scout, Rumford, was standing close by. He nodded pleasantly enough, but did not move from his place to welcome us more familiarly.

I had no difficulty in recognizing the principal figure in this company. The respectful attention with which he was regarded by the others enabled me to identify him at once. He was examining some papers as we walked in, and did not immediately lift his eyes. But his face was plainly visible, and I was struck by the firmness and resolution indicated in every feature. I should have been much better satisfied to discover some sign from which I might hope for a lenient judgment of my misdeed. At that moment I saw nothing but an embodiment of grim austerity.

He kept us waiting only a minute. Looking up, he said, aside, to the scout:

"So these are Claiborne's twins?"

Then he greeted my father, with somewhat formal precision:

"Good-evening, Colonel Claiborne. I congratulate you on having your children with you again."

"Thank you, general," said my father. "It is a great relief. With one single exception, all my personal anxieties are now at an end."

"What is the exception, colonel?"

"I must know what disposition will be made of my son's case before I can be at ease."

"I understand. His conduct has been reported to me by trustworthy witnesses. What do you expect for him?"

"I have not heard all the details, general. I don't know what to expect."

"Perhaps I ought to say, What would you wish?"

I perceived that my father was greatly discomposed, though he remained outwardly impassive. Few of those present would have conceived how painful the suspense was to him.

"If I may express a wish," he said, "it is that his youth and the impulse under which he acted may be taken into account. The Southern officer had rescued him from a horrible death, and this obligation made the boy unmindful of his strict duty. I trust that the circumstances will be remembered in mitigation of his punishment."

"Punishment!" exclaimed the general, sitting upright in his chair, and staring at my father in blank astonishment; "what are you speaking of? We are at cross-purposes. Rumford, come here."

The scout leaned down, and several sentences were exchanged between him and the head of the army in too subdued a tone to be heard at our distance. At the end of this colloquy the general turned to us again, and I fancied I saw a slight relaxation of the determined lines in his countenance.

" Now I have the whole of it." he said. " Your son concocted a scheme for the escape of a Southern officer."

"So I am informed," replied my father.

"You admit this, young gentleman?" proceeded the general, addressing me.

"It is true, sir."

Neither my father nor I would have thought it wise to add another word; but Jennie, poor child, who had all along been convinced that she had put the idea into my head, could not control herself.

" Ah, general," she faltered, "it was at my request he did it."

"Against his own will?" asked the general, stiffly.

"I think not," she answered; and then, more faintly, "I *hope* not."

"Hush, my daughter," said father. "What Lionel did, he must abide by."

A pause followed, which seemed to me interminable; and while it lasted we were curiously observed by all in the room. Finally the general's clear and even voice broke the silence.

"The escape of a prisoner is sometimes a dangerous matter. The least I can do, Colonel Claiborne, is to see that such a thing does not occur in your family again. The question is how to prevent it. Your son has placed a personal obligation above a public duty. We must put him in a position where that will be impossible. Under proper military discipline he will learn to regulate his feelings by the rules of the service. A lieutenant's commission is what he requires first of all. You will look after the rest."

I could hardly believe my ears. If the general was in earnest—and he seemed incapable of levity—I was to receive, instead of chastisement, a reward of high honor. It was incredible. I looked for the effect of what we had heard upon my father and sister. Jennie evidently did not comprehend it in the least. She was as much in the dark as little Julius, and a great deal more frightened. My father, too, was deeply agitated, but by a very different emotion. I had never before seen him so shaken from his usual placidity. He went forward hastily to a position nearer his chief.

"This is more than I could have hoped," he said, with much feeling. "I have done nothing to entitle me to such generosity."

"We will leave you out of consideration just now, colonel," answered General Grant. "I am settling accounts with your son. It appears that you have heard only a part of what he has done. He has told you about his transgression, but kept his gallant exploit to himself. All the more creditable to him. No, colonel, there's no generosity in this business. We are indebted to him for an important service. Like his father, he knows how to prove his loyalty at the right time. It runs in the Claiborne blood, I suppose."

If I may judge by my own sensations, the Claiborne blood stood still in all our veins when the captor of Vicksburg ceased speaking. Before any of us could recover ourselves, the general beckoned the lad whose presence I have mentioned, and said to him:

" Go and shake hands with that young gentleman, Fred. He will grow up to be a fine soldier."

The youth crossed the room and gave me his hand with frank boyish cordiality.

" I'm glad to hear that you belong to *us*," he said, brightly and cheerily.

Most of the company laughed at his quaint manner of welcoming me as a comrade in the service to which he considered himself attached, and the general's face was lighted with a smile which banished all the severity from his features. It was gone in an instant, but I have never forgotten that sudden and brief gleam of sunshine upon a countenance from which the expression of unbending gravity was so rarely absent.

I am sure that he introduced his son into the conversation with a thoughtful desire to relieve us, and particularly my father, from the strain and embarrassment of the situation. I told the lad I should value his kind congratulations, and then, approaching the general, offered him my thanks in words which I can only hope were befitting, for I do not recall a single one of them. After I had spoken, Jennie and Julius were brought up and presented by Master Fred, who, perceiving that they were under some constraint, gave them the benefit of his protection, and did his best to make them comfortable.

" I can't do better than dismiss you now," said General Grant, after a few casual sentences had

been exchanged. "You have yet a great deal
to hear and to tell, and would like to be alone,
no doubt. I will send Rumford around in the
course of the evening to supply some information
about the Helena battle which I find has not
been communicated to Lieutenant Claiborne."

Lieutenant Claiborne! The title took my
breath away. What was the "mister" of General Prentiss to this? An empty, insignificant
sound—nothing more. This had indeed a meaning! And my father, after he had heard all,
partly from me and partly from Rumford, was
pleased to declare that I deserved it. With a
heart full of gratitude and happiness I resolved
that my constant study should be to make myself more and more worthy of it, and to justify,
by unceasing industry and devotion, the confidence with which I had been so signally favored.

The events of a single Fourth of July thus introduced me to a career which I followed with
enthusiasm while the war lasted, and from which
I did not retire until called to another sphere of
duty. The Fourth of 1864 was passed at a
point far remote from our Arkansas home, but
the succeeding anniversary saw us under the old
roof once more, with our faithful little band of
retainers revelling around us. From that time
the history of the Claiborne family has been one

of peace and domestic prosperity. The even tranquillity of five-and-twenty years has been varied by so few exciting events that the episodes of the Rebellion, in which we were so actively concerned, sound like romantic fiction to the youthful generation now advancing to maturity. It is for the edification of these children of a less stormy period that I, the soldier of the past and the simple farmer of to-day, have undertaken to set down in lasting form the record of our share in the great contest between North and South. The juvenile circle for which it is intended has many members, all alike dear to us who watch the progress of their young lives; yet I have in this instance allowed myself to be so far partial as to dedicate my chronicle especially to two of the number, for no other reason than that they happen to be called Jennie and Lionel. They are not twins, however, and their last name is not Claiborne, but one which my sister has borne since her wedding day, when she ceased to be known in society as Miss Jennie Claiborne, and, with the heartiest approval of her father and brothers, became Mrs. Richard Fairchild. In these later years it is only her oldest and nearest relations who, looking back to the time of her youth, claim and exercise the right to speak of her as one of Claiborne's Twins.

GRACIE'S GODSON

I

First you shall learn how two babies — so called or miscalled — were made acquainted with each other under strange and anomalous conditions; and afterwards how one of them, by most unusual processes, but greatly to his happiness, became the other's godson.

Mrs. George Sheldon stood at an open window of her house in one of the far up-town districts of New York, looking across a little grass-plot which belonged to the establishment, and gravely inspecting the antics of a crowd of boys who were noisily amusing themselves on the sidewalk. She was in great distress. Her daughter Grace, a child five years of age, lay dangerously ill up-stairs—so ill that the doctor doubted her chance of recovery unless she could be kept in perfect rest and quiet for several days to come.

Mr. Sheldon had ordered tan to be spread in the street to deaden the sound of passing vehicles, and within-doors the utmost silence was maintained day and night. But there was one cause of disturbance which had just that afternoon made itself apparent, and against which the anxious mother felt herself unable to contend.

The street urchins of that neighborhood were as bad a rabble as could be found in any except the most disreputable quarters of the city. Fine residences were gradually crowding out the rude hovels which originally covered the ground, but numbers of wretched shanties still remained, occupied by an extremely low and ill-regulated class of tenants. The proportion of children among these seemed entirely beyond reasonable calculation. They swarmed through the thoroughfares at all hours, bent upon nothing but finding ways of making themselves obnoxious and destroying the peace of decent citizens. No form of diversion was satisfactory to them in which they could not contribute to the annoyance and exasperation of the orderly community. Clamor and confusion were essential to their happiness, and he who could discover the newest methods of creating uproar became the temporary leader in their pastimes and the idol of his mates.

A handsome fence of iron bars separated the Sheldons' little lawn from the sidewalk. It is a matter of notorious record that, since the earliest dawn of history, fences of this description have been choice objects of interest and affection to boys of every station and degree, their rooted conviction being that such structures are fabricated solely to afford them the unspeakable delight of dragging sticks along the parallel spokes from end to end, thereby producing a clangor like that of a watchman's rattle multiplied and aggravated a hundred-fold. To the very best of boys the temptation to indulge in this exhilarating sport is almost irresistible. By the boys of the locality in which the Sheldons dwelt it would have been deemed a wilful if not a criminal neglect of opportunity — a flying in the face of beneficent fortune—to refrain from revelling in the luxury which circumstance had placed at their disposal. The only wonder was that they had not found it out before, and turned it to happy account.

Now, however, the entertainment was in vigorous operation, and the performers were making up for the time lost during the period when the splendid possibilities of iron pickets were yet unrevealed to them. The master of ceremonies was a youth somewhat smaller in stature and

presumably younger than the majority of his
companions, who carried in his right hand a steel
rod about two feet long, which he pressed with
all his force against the bars as he ran the whole
length of the fence, making a din sufficient to
shatter the senses of a rhinoceros, not to speak
of the delicate nerves of the little sick girl. He
was closely followed by a dozen or more juvenile
vagabonds, some with barrel-staves, some with
broom-handles, some with sections of stove-fun-
nels. Several of the party carried two clattering
contrivances, one in each fist. The commander-
in-chief was debarred this privilege, being under
the necessity of holding a bundle of newspapers
to his side with his left arm, but the energy and
dexterity with which he manipulated the steel
rod gave him a superiority which could not justly be contested, and made him easily the first
among his fellows — *facile princeps*, he would
have been called had he been a gutter imp of
ancient Rome instead of an unruly newsboy of
modern New York.

What could Mrs. Sheldon do? She might send
for a policeman, and have the mischievous mob
dispersed, but she well knew that the relief thus
obtained would be merely momentary. The officer's back would no sooner be turned than the
pests would be at their work again, strengthened

"THE ENTERTAINMENT WAS IN VIGOROUS OPERATION"

with reinforcements and stimulated by revenge-
ful wrath to fresh exertions. The unhappy lady
was in torture at the thought of what her darling
might be suffering from the hideous tumult. She
understood how useless would be any attempt to
bribe the malefactors to peace and quiet. Pity
was not in their nature. They would have taken
her money, and then spread the intelligence that
instantaneous wealth was at the command of any
body of boys who chose to seek it through this
fascinating channel. The nuisance would simply
be intensified and prolonged.

While she gazed, more in sorrow than in anger, at the persecutors of her baby, the director
of the discordant orchestra chanced to turn in
her direction, and caught sight of her face at the
raised window. This young scapegrace was not
without some of the qualities of an estimable
lady immortalized by a famous poet of the last
century: "Though on pleasure he was bent, he
had a frugal mind." He checked himself abruptly in his furious race up and down the sidewalk, and pushing open the gate, ran across the
lawn and planted himself directly in front of
Mrs. Sheldon.

"Papeers!" he cried. "Evening papeers!
Wor-yeeld! Sun! Tel'gram!"

The lady shook her head without speaking.

"Extree!" persisted the peddler of news.
"*Wor-yeeld*—sport'n edish'n! *Mail 'n' Expray-ess !*"

Receiving no encouragement, he whirled swift-ly upon his heels, right willing to relinquish the shadowy hope of commerce with a stranger for the certainty of resuming a delightful recreation with his comrades.

"Oh, baby! baby!" exclaimed Mrs. Sheldon, sadly, as he started away with a flourish of his metal rod in the air.

Unexpectedly to her he swung round again and looked up with an impudent stare of in-quiry.

"No," she said; "I want no papers."

"Yer called me," he returned, sulkily.

"I did not call," she replied.

"Yes, yer did. Yer sung out 'Baby.'"

"Is your name Baby?" Mrs. Sheldon asked, with indifference, not caring in the least wheth-er it was or not.

"O' course it ain't; but that's what the fellers calls me—choke 'em! Just wait till I get a year bigger. Then I'll 'Baby' every father's son of 'em!"

Mrs. Sheldon now looked at the boy more at-tentively than before, and what she saw im-pressed her. He was about twelve years old,

raggedly clad, and as untidy as those of his calling are apt to be. His attitude was defiant, and
the expression of his countenance was hard and
aggressive. But the features were as fine and
delicate as those of a girl, and the dirt on his
cheeks could not hide the clear brightness of his
complexion. In his red tangled hair there was
a shine of gold, and his large blue eyes gleamed
with a light the charm of which went far to
counteract the vicious boldness of their stare.
It seemed probable to the observant lady that
the title of "Baby" had been bestowed by his
associates in consequence of his peculiar beauty,
which they regarded as effeminate and infantile,
and that he resented the imputations it conveyed
with the spirit becoming to an advanced newsboy of the nineteenth century.

The thought came rapidly to her mind that
the epithet applied in mockery might possibly
have some justification in the lad's character;
and if this were the case, an appeal to his better
feeling on behalf of her afflicted child might not
be utterly fruitless. It was a slender hope, but
she would make the trial.

"I'll buy your papers," she said.

"How many of 'em?"

"All you have, if you will do what I desire.
Come into the house; I will open the door."

8

"What's the game?" he demanded, with a sharp glance of distrust.

"Come, if you wish to sell your papers. If not, I can wait here no longer."

"Yer won't go to set a watch-dog on me?" he said, hesitating. "I can't fight a watch-dog."

By way of reply she drew a portemonnaie from her pocket, and took out some loose silver. The glitter of the coin appeared to allay his suspicions, and when she threw back the hall door he walked jauntily in, with considerably more effrontery in his air than was natural or appropriate to the situation.

"What is your real name?" inquired Mrs. Sheldon, leading the way to the room in which she had been standing.

"Dun' no'," was the reply, in a sullen tone.

"Surely you are not always called Baby?"

"Down at the newspaper shops they calls me the Coyote."

"Indeed! And which do you like best?"

"By-'n'-by I'm goin' to strip the hide off of every feller what's called me Baby—if I kin."

"Very well; it doesn't matter whether you have a name or not. Now take off your cap."

"What 'll I do with it?" demanded the young scamp, looking furtively and warily about him. He obeyed, however, and held the tattered head-covering awkwardly in his hand, with a look of surprise at being thus required to encumber himself, when any one might see that to leave it in its natural and customary resting-place would be much more comfortable for all concerned.

"Put it in your pocket, if you like," said the lady; "anywhere except on your head."

He preferred to roll it up and poke it inside the breast of his flaring red woollen shirt, after which he proceeded to dishevel his hair with the unoccupied hand; but he could not brush away the rich coloring or straighten the kink out of the short curls.

"Listen to me," Mrs. Sheldon continued. "Have you a mother or a sister?"

"No," he answered, without a sign of interest.

"Have you ever been sick?"

"Guess not; don't remember."

"I have a little girl — scarcely more than a baby — who is very sick, perhaps dying. The least noise hurts her terribly. Can you stop that dreadful banging on the fence?"

"What 'll yer give me to stop?"

"I don't mean you alone; I want you to keep the others quiet, too."

"How kin I do that?" he asked, impatiently.

"If you tell them why, perhaps they will go away."

"O' course they won't," he rejoined, scornfully. "Catch 'em!"

The sorrowful mother was reluctant to let the
chance slip by, poor as it was. If this small rag-
amuffin had a spark of humanity in him, it ought
to be touched by the anguish of her child. It
was hard to believe that a boy of his years could
be wholly insensible to compassion. Suddenly
she resolved to bring him face to face with the
little invalid up-stairs.

"Come and look at my dear daughter," she
said. "When you see how weak and ill she is,
you will understand why I ask you to help me.
Step softly, and do not speak out loud."

II

WITHOUT a word the newsboy followed her to
the floor above, and walked unmoved into the
chamber where the ailing girl lay. A nurse who
was sitting at the bedside looked up astonished
at the unexpected visitor, but Mrs. Sheldon imposed silence by a gesture, and beckoned him to
draw near.

It needed no keen perception to realize the
sufferer's condition. Her gentle face was hag-

gard with pain, and her soft dark eyes seemed to plead for relief as she turned them beseechingly upon her mother.

"Mamma," she moaned, feebly, "please do make them stop; my head aches so."

"I am going to try, dear," Mrs. Sheldon answered. To the boy she added in an undertone: "You can see what misery she is in. When you tell your playfellows they will surely listen."

"Do no good," he muttered. "Gi' me a minute to think. May I look out o' winder?"

"Yes. We have to keep it open all the time, the heat is so great. You can hear how frightful the noise is."

He crept across the room, and peered cautiously forth. While he did this the nurse, who regarded him with extreme disfavor, said to Mrs. Sheldon,

"Don't trust that wretch for anything, ma'am; he'll be a great deal readier to do harm than good."

"He has a beautiful face, nurse."

"But the wickedness of his eyes is awful. There's nothing but spitefulness in him."

She would have continued in the same strain if the object of her disparagement had not quickly returned and interrupted her. He was smiling in a peculiar and by no means amiable way.

"I'm the feller that kin do it," he said, with a hoarse chuckle. "What's the figure?"

"You ought to be ashamed of yourself," the nurse broke in, very earnestly, though as softly as possible. "You ought to be overjoyed to do anything in the world for this dear, unhappy little angel."

"This is biz," he retorted, with an ugly scowl. "The lady promised to buy all my papers."

"That is true," assented Mrs. Sheldon; "and I will do it, and a great deal more, if you can drive those boys out of the street."

"I've got the trick," he responded, leering craftily. "I know how to work it straight through, if yer come down handsome, and make it worth my while. Yer've only got to leave it to me, and it goes. Put up the cash, and I'll clear 'em all out, sure as I stand here. I kin send 'em spinning soon as I like, or," he whispered, with a malicious grin, "I kin keep 'em at it harder'n ever all day long and p'r'aps all night. 'Tain't for me to say which it's goin' to be. It's for you to choose, ma'am, and make up yer mind how much yer'll stand."

Mrs. Sheldon looked at the heartless young reprobate with unconcealed disgust. The nurse was for a moment speechless with indignation, but quickly recovering the use of her tongue, she said,

"SHE ADDED, IN AN UNDERTONE, ' YOU CAN SEE WHAT MISERY SHE IS IN'"

"Don't give him a cent, ma'am, I beg of you; not unless he proves that he can do what you wish."

"I will pay for your papers in any case," Mrs. Sheldon remarked, coldly; "that was agreed. If you stop this hideous crashing, you shall have— Give attention, if you please."

She paused, observing that he was casting sharp glances about the room and curiously inspecting the furniture, instead of listening as closely as she thought necessary.

"I'm a-hearin' of yer," he replied. "Go ahead, ma'am."

"If you make them stop now, you shall come to me this evening at nine o'clock for half a dollar. If they are quiet all day to-morrow you shall have another half-dollar at the same hour."

"It's too much, Mrs. Sheldon," protested the nurse.

"Not if he succeeds. And so on every day until my child is well."

"S'pose she don't get well?"

"You unfeeling little monster, how dare you?" said the nurse, writhing under the necessity of keeping her ire within bounds. "Of course she will get well."

"Oh, I dare say, 'cause *you're* a-nursin' of her," was the sneering response. "Well, I didn't mean for her to hear, anyway. So that's the bargain, ma'am. I'm to have half a dollar for every day the fellers don't play onto the fence!"

"Yes; and my thanks, if you care for them."

It did not appear that he was dazzlingly allured by this part of the prospective reward. His eyes began to rove around the chamber again, as if attracted by the various unfamiliar objects distributed here and there. All at once he said: "Will yer let me look into the street once more?"

Mrs. Sheldon nodded in assent, and for a minute he devoted himself to a second scrutiny of the window, after which he returned apparently satisfied.

"The papers is thirty-five cents," he observed.

"I will count them, ma'am," proposed the nurse.

"Oh, go 'way!" the thrifty speculator grunted, in deep scorn and mockery. "Anybody kin see 'tain't *your* kid that's sick."

"Be quiet," ordered Mrs. Sheldon. "Here is the money, and you may keep the papers. They are of no use to me."

"May I?" he said, greedily; but, on reflection, he declined the offer, though with evident reluctance. "No, that 'll spoil my game. But if yer want to make me a present, I'll take it money down."

"Oh, ma'am, do send the jackanapes away," entreated the nurse. "He's only deceivin' you."

The jackanapes surveyed her with cool contempt, and, turning his back to the bed, addressed himself exclusively to the mistress of the house.

"I'll go now," he said. "Yer'll hear lots of music for the next five or ten minutes. Don't mind that. Shut the window if yer can't stand the racket. Yer'll see me goin' in louder'n any of 'em. That's all right; yer'll be able to hold out a little while longer, I guess. Then I'll come back to the house and pertend to talk to you. I sha'n't have nothing to say; just let me in, and pretty soon I'll clear out for good. If I can't fix the boys, nobody can't do it. Say, it's square about that half-dollar to-night?"

"You shall have it, if you earn it."

He pocketed the money that was handed to him, laid his bundle of papers on a chair, drew forth his cap and clapped it on the back of his head, made an apish grimace at the nurse, who watched the proceedings wrathfully, and betook himself down-stairs and into the open air.

III

Though her expectations had not much to rest upon, Mrs. Sheldon followed the newsboy's movements attentively through the window. For a time she saw little to encourage her.

The reappearance of their leader was the signal for an uproarious demonstration on the part of the juvenile mob. After the interchange of a few words, he sprang with redoubled vigor to his interrupted sport, using not only the formidable steel rod, but also an old saw blade, of which he ruthlessly dispossessed a smaller member of the brotherhood.

"He's the worst of them all," said the nurse, who had come to look on by her employer's side.

"He told me he should do this at first," answered Mrs. Sheldon, clinging to the faintest chance of a respite.

"Ah, ma'am, there's nothing on earth like their rascality."

"I thought he seemed less wild and brutal than they generally are, nurse. Did you notice that he spoke a little more correctly than most of them? He did not say 'de' and 'dat' for 'the' and 'that,' like many that you hear. Perhaps he has some ideas of right and wrong."

" Well, ma'am, it's my opinion the workin's of the human breast don't go by parts o' speech, nor yet the way you pronounce 'em. I've heard ladies that goes out to service make mistakes in a way with their mouths, and their hearts as good as California gold all day long."

A stronger brogue than usual accompanied the slight tone of injury in which the excellent Irish nurse delivered this piece of wisdom, and Mrs. Sheldon forbore further discussion of the delicate point. She was about to turn the conversation to subjects in which no tinge of personality could be suspected, when it was observed that the order of events without began to change. A number of the older boys suspended operations and withdrew from the line. They were seen to follow the Baby, and question him eagerly. He also paused, and allowed himself to be drawn into an animated conversation. But his inactivity did not last long ; he was quickly at work again, creating alone as much din as the half-dozen who had retired. Presently he was surrounded, and an attempt was made to drag him from the fence. This he resisted angrily, and a stormy debate ensued. His voice was heard loud above the rest, though what he said could not be distinguished.

At last he seemed to yield to the pressure put
upon him by the majority, and with every indication of repugnance and ill-humor he left the
crowd, and marched up the pathway to the house.
The commotion ceased as if by magic.

"He has actually stopped them," exclaimed
Mrs. Sheldon. "How could he do it?"

"Don't be too sure, ma'am," the nurse advised.
"It may be a trick to get the money sooner.
Pray don't give him any before night."

Mrs. Sheldon went to the door and admitted
the boy, who showed no disposition to respond
to her questions, saying merely that he guessed
the job was safe now, and that he would come
for his pay at nine o'clock.

"And then you will tell me how you persuaded
them," she proposed.

"Not much," he replied, winking slyly. "When
I get a good thing, I keep it to myself."

And indeed it was long before the lady, or any
of her family, learned the secret of his power to
control the actions of that lawless tribe.

The Baby, or the Coyote, as it less offended his
dignity to be designated, was a strategist. Outside of the narrow range of his obscure life and
class he knew nothing, but with the nature and
characteristics of his associates he was pretty
thoroughly acquainted. To this accurate under-

standing he owed the success of the scheme he
had devised for the abatement of Mrs. Sheldon's
grievance and his own pecuniary advantage.

When he came forth, after pledging himself to
undertake the difficult enterprise, he assumed an
air of dense preoccupation, scarcely heeding the
acclamations which greeted him. To the inquiries of his most intimate friends he vouchsafed
only the curtest replies.

"Where's your papes, Baby?"

"No use for 'em; got a bigger job on hand;"
and he wrenched the saw blade away from a
weaker brother, as heretofore described, and commenced a series of variations on the fence with
all the might of his soul and body.

This was mysterious, and a mystery is not the
sort of thing to be passed by the ordinary street
arab without probing. The big boys began to
transfer their interest from the pursuit of the
hour to their comrade's behavior. Without con-
sultation, but inspired by a common impulse, they
drew aside and studied him. So far as they could
perceive, he was entirely unconscious of this scrutiny, and they soon proceeded to more active and
direct methods of investigation.

"Say, Baby, what's up?"

"Gone out o' de newspaper biz, Baby?"

"Who's in wid yer on de new lay?"

"Got Vanderbilk for a pardner, Baby?"

These and similar inquiries received no attention, and the temper of the crowd went through a variety of hasty changes, until it rose to a state of high excitement. Then the Baby desisted from his labors and condescended to explain.

"See here, there's a lot o' sick kids in that house. Not very sick, but too sick to be let out. Nothin' them kids likes so much as rattlin' on these here rails. If they can't do it themselves, they hanker to hear it. Cry for it all day long. Just tickled to death when we started in this afternoon. Mother called me in, and offered me a half to keep it up till supper-time. What's papers to that? Oh yes; I guess not. You let me alone; I've struck it solid this stretch, I tell yer."

"Say, Baby, did she pay yer down?"

"Never you mind; the pay's all safe. Stand out o' the way there."

"Goin' to let us in, Baby, ain't yer?"

"What 'll I let yer in for? This job belongs to me."

"Ain't we goin' to get nothin' for what we've been doin'? We've been hard at work amusin' dem kids for nigh an hour. We don't go round serenadin' sick kids free gratis dis year, does we, fellers?"

"Not if we knows it," was the tenor of the general cry.

"Look a-here, Jim Broggins," said the Baby, addressing the tallest and leanest of the pack, and assuming an accent of wounded virtue, "what d'yer want to break me up for? Just you go along and spot a house for yerself that's got sick kids into it. I ain't a-tryin' to crowd you out nowhere."

"Oh, ain't yer?" rejoined the lank Broggins. "Well, we ain't agoin' to be crowded out here, neider. What d'yer say, fellers? We've been buildin' up a business all de afternoon, and as soon as it begins to pay, de Baby he waltzes in and scoops de profits. Wants to play it on us, he does. Well, it don't go. Yer've got to square wid us Baby, or we'll *make* yer keep still, anyway."

A loud chorus of assent attested the universal agreement in this decision, and the Baby, artfully allowing his countenance to fall, appeared greatly dejected.

"What's the good of half a dollar among a dozen of us?" he said, moodily.

"No good at all," answered Broggins, promptly. "She's got to give more. De idea of expectin' us to entertain a lot o' lazy kids at dat cheap figure. You go and fix it, Baby."

"No use," objected the wily speculator, shaking his head emphatically.

"Den *you'll* shut up shop, dat's all."

"Tell yer what I'll do, Jim Broggins," the young diplomatist said, after a moment of pretended meditation. "Step over here, you and our partic'lar chums."

He beckoned half a dozen of his special allies, and confided to them privately that while it was out of the question to look for any such remuneration as would satisfy the entire assemblage, there was a possibility that he might persuade the lady to give enough for the needs of a select committee like themselves. For the small fry it would not matter. They could be frozen out. If they put on airs, they should be summarily dealt with. He would do his best to get the terms fixed at a quarter apiece for the six of them, and if any fellow thought he could drive a better bargain, let him go up and try.

"Go it, Baby; you're de daisy!" shouted Broggins; and his sentiments were enthusiastically echoed by the new combination.

In supposed pursuance of this object, the delegate returned to the house and held his brief second interview with Mrs. Sheldon. When he came forth again, the gloom of unutterable woe and disappointment was stamped upon his brow.

"What's up, Baby? Won't she come to time?"

"She's a stiff 'un, fellers. Said she'd set her dog on me, if she warn't afraid my clothes would p'ison him."

"What for?"

"I told her the whole story, and said we'd do it up handsome for a dollar 'n' a half all round, every afternoon. She just stuck out her chin and made faces. Then I asked her what she'd agree to, and she said half a dollar, and no more. I told her we couldn't afford it, nohow; that we'd got an organization and would go on strike, every one of us, if she didn't meet us fair and liberal. I thought that would scare her, but she up and laughed. 'I kin git a boy any time to do it for a half, or less,' says she. 'Bet yer what yer like yer can't,' says I, 'not when we're on strike.' 'Why not?' says she. 'Cause we'll up and bycutt him,' says I. 'What d'yer mean by that?' says she. 'Why,' says I, 'we'll roll him in the gutter and scrub him with brick-bats if he tries it on.' 'Oh,' says she, 'that's bycuttin, is it?' 'That's the size of it,' says I, 'only sometimes it's bigger.' 'Well,' says she, 'I kin buy all the fence music I want for half a dollar a day, and you may consider yourself discharged.' 'Good enough, ma'am,' says I; 'you an' yer kids 'll have no more fun out o' them iron railin's till yer plank

9

down.' Then she went sassy, and let on about the
dog, and insulted me clothes, and I got out in a
hurry. But never mind, fellers. Let her find
out we're in earnest, and she'll have to give in.
Do what I tell yer, and we're dead sure to win
this trick."

IV

A WILD howl of rage bore testimony that the
orator had rightly estimated the spirit of his
party. After a very brief deliberation it was
unanimously resolved that no sound of cheerful
clangór should be permitted to arise from the
fence from that time forth. The "kids" should
have none of their favorite lullaby until the
mother was prepared to pay for it at the fair
and reasonable valuation stipulated by the committee through their authorized representative.
The league of six was divided into sections for
patrol duty, and in case of any attempt by a
stranger, or by the smaller boys of the present
crowd, to perform at reduced prices to the injury
of the union, an alarm was to be given, and a
general rally called for the suppression of cheap
labor. This state of things was to be maintained
for a week, or longer if necessary; but it was

felt that grinding capital, in the person of the lady of the house, could not hold out more than a day or two in face of the opposition organized and directed by the newsboy and his indignant retinue.

At nine o'clock in the evening the Baby, careful to avoid detection by his mates, presented himself, according to appointment, at Mrs. Sheldon's door. He was admitted by a servant, who, under instructions, led him once again to the sick-chamber. The fond mother could not doubt that it would gratify the boy to be received there — to witness for himself the beneficial change brought about by a few hours of undisturbed repose, and to be rewarded by the little girl's acknowledgments, as well as her own. She hoped that he would thus be inspired to renewed exertions on behalf of the patient for whose welfare he was striving, at least in part. It did not seem credible to her loving heart that even the most abandoned of his class could look upon that frail and delicate creature without being touched by sympathy and stirred by unselfish emotions. She believed, moreover, that by this unusual mark of confidence she could appeal to the sense of humanity that must be lingering somewhere within him, and in this manner confer a better return for his service than that of the

mere payment in money. It would have been
hard to convince her that all these fancies were
based upon an entirely misplaced faith, and that
it was utterly beyond her power to kindle a
spark of generosity in that hardened and unen-
lightened soul. A face like his, she told herself
too trustfully, surely could not represent a wholly
evil mind.

The invalid was wide awake when he entered,
and as he stepped to the bedside he pulled off
his cap with a quick movement, and deposited it,
as before, in the bosom of his shirt. Either he
remembered the admonition of the afternoon, or
a new instinct of propriety had dawned upon
him. He did not open his mouth, but waited for
some other person to break the silence.

"Gracie dear," said Mrs. Sheldon, "here is the
little boy who stopped the noise in the street for
you. We could have done nothing without him."

The child fixed her eyes earnestly upon him
before replying.

"I'm so glad," she presently murmured. "It
did hurt me dreadfully, mamma."

"Won't you thank him for the pains he took?"
continued Mrs. Sheldon.

"He knows I thank him," answered Gracie;
"of course he knows."

"I thank you too," said the mother. "We are

all grateful. She could not sleep until you sent the boys away. You can see how much good you have done."

"Will he always be as good?" inquired Gracie.

"Ask him, dear."

"Will you?" said the child, again turning her gaze upon him.

He glanced first at Gracie, and then at Mrs. Sheldon, with a very uneasy expression. This sort of questioning was not in his calculations. Were they trying to make him forget that they owed him half a dollar? No; the little girl was too sick to be put up to any such trick as that. She wasn't the kind, either, to play shabby games on a fellow. What eyes she had — how big and bright; though it was the disease, to be sure, that made them so big and bright. He wondered how they looked when she was well. Did she speak that way when she was up and running about—so soft and chirpy? "Just like a bird might," he thought, "if a bird could say things."

"Will you be good again, and not have any noise to-morrow?" asked Gracie, once more.

The boy nodded his head affirmatively, but gave no response in words. Possibly he was conscious of the absurdity of binding himself by a ridiculous pledge to "be good," though ready to adhere to the more practical part of his agreement.

"He has promised, dear; I know he will," said Mrs. Sheldon. "And now say good-night; you mustn't talk any more."

"Good-night," repeated Gracie, smiling at him from her pillow. "Come again soon."

He seemed on the point of answering in some fashion, when the nurse walked into the room and uttered an exclamation of discontent at seeing him. Instantly his face grew dark and morose, and he drew away, muttering, "Gi' me my half-dollar and let me go."

Mrs. Sheldon went for the money to a toilet-stand in a corner, upon which several pieces of jewelry were lying exposed. The boy followed her movements with a strained attention. Had she perceived the fierce avidity with which his eyes rested upon the flashing gems, she would have hesitated to indulge the kindly purposes she had in view, and recognized the weakness of attempting reclamation by any means at her command. But her amiable disposition prompted her to judge all who came near with the utmost charity; and even in this extreme case she could make no exception.

For several successive days the Baby maintained his hold upon her consideration by the

thoroughness with which he performed the duty
he had assumed. It needed all the ingenuity he
could exercise to preserve discipline among his
disorderly band, but through a full week he succeeded in keeping their expectations alive, and
persuading them that their true policy was to
wait for overtures from the other side. At the
end of this time Gracie's recovery was so nearly
assured that Mrs. Sheldon's worst apprehensions
had disappeared. The child would soon be well
enough to be removed to the country, and the
noises of the street were no longer likely to cause
her serious injury.

V

THE Baby came regularly each evening for his
stipend. Once or twice he was seen by Mr.
Sheldon, who chaffed him to a point of high
irritation. Mr. Sheldon also chaffed his wife,
declaring that she had been duped by a midget
of an impostor; that a word to the police would
have accomplished everything the tatterdemalion
pretended to secure; and that the warm-hearted
lady had simply been carried away by the delu-
sive good looks of the young scamp, and cajoled

into the belief that he was better than the average of his order by the light of his large blue eyes, the glow of his complexion, and the glitter of his golden hair. But Mr. Sheldon knew perfectly well all the while that the protection of the police could have been obtained in such a matter only at great trouble and cost, if at all; and he was, in fact, well contented to avail himself of the newsboy's agency, without inquiring too curiously as to the methods employed. He was correct, however, in his supposition that the lad was no better than the average of his tribe. He might have gone a great deal further. The Baby was not only much worse than the average, but, through corrupt associations and debasing influences, had reached a depth of badness below which it would scarcely have been possible for him to descend.

Throughout the whole of his unhappy life the poor outcast had had no chance. He knew nothing of his father or mother, and had never heard even his own name. He had grown to his present age in the midst of the most depraved surroundings, and been taught to believe that the only natural laws were those of self-preservation and indiscriminate pillage. In conformity to these, he kept no earthly end in view but the immediate satisfaction of his individual necessities. He was a newsboy not especially by inclination, but because this calling helped him in the easiest way to a livelihood. He would have preferred to steal, and meant to when he grew older, but the time for adopting that agreeable and exciting vocation as a regular career had not yet arrived. If opportunities presented themselves, however, there was no reason why he should not turn them to account; and unless he was greatly mistaken, one of the prime opportunities of his life was now beckoning him to improve it.

What had hitherto stood most in the way of his ambition was the deplorable effeminacy of his personal appearance. With the spirit of a man, as he imagined, he was disgraced by the exterior of a girl. He would have given anything to exchange the good looks which by some freak of circumstance clung to him through all vicissitudes for the utmost coarseness and ungainliness that nature could provide. When he was younger he had lain awake nights fretting over this irremediable misfortune. For a while he would not admit to himself that it was irremediable. He was not prepared to go to the length of damaging his sight or destroying the usefulness of his teeth, but he ardently envied the bleared eyes and tobacco-stained fangs of the

"toughs" whom he admired. He did his best
to hide the odious red and white of his skin
under coatings of grime, and tortured his inven-
tion to discover schemes for reducing his hair to
subjection. This was the severest of his trials.
He once prevailed upon a friendly shoeblack to
"shine his head up" and put a first-class five-
cent polish on his tawny mane, but the result
was not sufficiently lasting to be thoroughly approved. A companion fertile in suggestion proposed shaving his crown and pricking india-ink
into the scalp, but it could not be shown that
this expedient had ever been successfully prac-
tised, and it was dismissed without a test. It
might be true, the Baby admitted, that you
could take the curl out of a puppy's tail by cut-
ting it off, but that was because the tail would
not grow again, whereas a boy's hair would
grow; and it was a question which never could
be answered to his satisfaction, whether the curl
in his case was not a more burdensome affliction
than the color.

During all his visits to the sick girl's chamber the young rogue's thoughts were bent upon
plunder. His quick sight had caught the glim-
mer of the jewels upon the toilet-stand, and he
had listened greedily to the statement that the
windows were left open at all times. He had

observed that a trellis thinly covered with vines
was affixed to the front of the house, and after
diligent examination from without and within it
was plain to him that no extraordinary agility
would be required to effect a secret entrance.
He did not know whether the little invalid was
ever left alone at night, but this he would endeavor to learn. At any rate, there would probably be no wide-awake watch kept when she
began to get really better.

On his second evening call Gracie greeted her
odd visitor almost like an acquaintance. With
her pretty smile and pleasant voice she bade him
welcome, and told him she was ever so obliged
for the quiet and comfortable day he had given
her. As before, he manifested no desire to be
sociable; but since it was to his advantage to
make himself as familiar as possible with the locality, he thought it well to prolong his stay by
entering into conversation.

"What is your name?" asked Gracie, as he
stood looking stolidly at her.

"Nem'mind my name," he said; less gruffly,
however, than when Mrs. Sheldon had put the
same question.

"But you must tell me," insisted the child.
"How can I talk to you if I don't know your
name?"

"Well, some folks calls me Baby," he replied, half sheepishly, half defiantly.

"Why, that's what mamma and papa often call me!" exclaimed Gracie. "How funny!"

"That's all right," the boy exclaimed. "You *are* a baby; I'm a man!"

"Oh!" said Gracie, somewhat doubtfully. "But you ought to have a name, and Baby belongs to me. I shall call you Robin."

"Why Robin, dear?" her mother inquired.

"Because his face is like my picture of Robin Goodfellow, and he has been good to me; that's one reason. Then look at him, mamma—he's all red, just like a real robin; don't you see?"

The Baby mumbled in a manner denoting dissatisfaction. The compliment made no impression on him, and the allusion to his distinguishing hue offended his pride. Still, if she wanted to call him Robin, why not? It sounded nice and comfortable, as she said it, and, so far as he could judge, it was an improvement upon either of his more familiar titles.

From that time he was Robin to the child and to all who saw him in the Sheldon house, saving the nurse, whose aversion never diminished, and who refused to speak of him except as "the brat" to the servants, and "that saucebox" to her employers. Her hostility did not make it appear

at all necessary to Mrs. Sheldon that he be ex-
cluded from the premises.   She was pleased with
anything in which her darling found even a trifling interest, and she also continued to harbor
the fancy that it was for the good of the wayward vagrant to breathe, if only for once or
twice in his life, an atmosphere made pure and
wholesome by influences unknown in the sphere
to which he belonged.

VI

FOR six consecutive evenings the newsboy re-
appeared, always receiving his half-dollar, although towards the end he displayed an unac-
countable reluctance, to taking the money in
Gracie's presence.   On his last regular arrival
he was informed that the nurse was no longer in
attendance.   This satisfied him on more grounds
than one.   He detested her cordially, in the first
place, and he also knew that her absence would
facilitate the execution of the difficult scheme
which he was planning.   Already he was on
fairly easy terms with the child, and the assurance that his particular enemy was out of the
way made him quite cheerful.

"I'm all well now, Robin," said Gracie. "Mamma won't let me get up yet, but I'm truly well. You ought to be glad of that."

"So I am," he replied, shortly.

"Mamma thought once that I was going to die."

"Oh no; guess not."

"She did, and so did you. I heard you say it, Robin."

He felt his face flush and scorch him, at which he was very angry. "Didn't mean to," he growled.

"But I knew you were sorry," she said, consolingly. "Never mind; I shall soon be as strong as ever. Nurse has gone, and I'm going to sleep alone every night."

"Shouldn't think they'd let yer," he whispered, glancing stealthily round at Mrs. Sheldon, who was busy in another part of the chamber.

"Why, yes, I always do when I'm not sick. Of course papa and mamma are in the next room, and the door stays open."

"O' course."

"And a fortnight from to-morrow we shall go to the country, if I am able to travel so soon."

The boy started, and looked keenly into her face. He had not hitherto given himself time to follow out all the consequences of her re-covery.

"A fortnight from to-morrow — Friday," he said, slowly. "That 'll be the 1st of August, I reckon."

"I don't know. You'll come and see me be-fore then?"

"I'll come if yer mother's willin'."

"Indeed she will be. Mamma, Robin must promise."

The mother made no objection. He under-stood, however, that the nightly calls were not to be continued. Mr. Sheldon had notified him that, as the term of his contract was at an end, the daily allowance of fifty cents would be stopped; but had added that in case there should be no renewal of the street disturbances during the next two weeks, he might look for a good round sum—say five dollars. The Baby knew perfectly well that there would be no more trou-ble with the fence. The boys had grown tired of the business, and had chosen another locality for their playground. He was not such an idiot, however, as to give this fact away to the Shel-dons. He told them he should have to be on watch all day long, that it was the toughest job he ever put his fist to, and that it was wearing the flesh off his bones. Oh yes, the money

would be well earned, and he would turn up
without fail at the right time to get it.

After obtaining all requisite information on
this point, the Baby withdrew. He was particularly grumpy about accepting the last half-
dollar which Mrs. Sheldon proffered him, and
snappishly refused to recognize its existence until he was out of Gracie's room. But he took it
readily enough then, and would have taken a
dozen more with all the pleasure in life if he
could have laid his hands upon them.

The fortnight went by, and he again stood, at
a late hour of the evening, by Gracie's bedside.
Many times during the interval he had prowled
about the neighborhood after dark ; but he had
taken good care to escape observation, and, indeed, had not usually commenced his wanderings
until after respectable citizens had gone to sleep.
No one in the house suspected how constant and
vigilant his attendance had been.

" How long it is since I have seen you, Robin!"
said the child. " I have missed you."

It was quite true. The rough boy of the
streets had an attraction for the delicately nurt-
ured girl, which could be explained only upon
the principle that the sharpest contrasts are
often the most closely drawn together. Her
mother thought that she regarded him with the

same interest she would have felt in a big, shaggy, handsome dog or pony. Gracie was fond of animals, and this was not the first time that her fancy had been caught by an out-of-the-way living plaything.

"Yer father said I was to come to-night," answered the Baby.

"But you needn't have stayed away *all* the time. I'm going to-morrow, and you don't know when you will see me again."

"I sha'n't never see yer no more," he declared.

"Yes, you will, you foolish Robin. You can come in the.morning and wish me good-bye, and after I get back in the fall you'll *always* see me."

He shook his head, saying to himself it was no use taking notice of such nonsense. He did expect to see her once—just once—but she would not see him, or know anything about it. A pretty mess if she should!

"Just think of not coming to see me," she resumed, "after helping me to get well!"

"D'yer s'pose I did help?"

"Be sure you did, you naughty boy. Mamma says you kept everything still in the street ever so many days, so that I could sleep and rest. Don't you know that?"

"Oh yes, I know a lot," he replied, with a bitter vehemence which he could not himself ac-

10

count for, and which he had no sort of doubt
was wholly unnecessary and stupid.

"Well, *I* sha'n't forget it, Robin; not ever."

She gave him a bright smile, which in some
way made him uncomfortable. She had smiled
at him often enough before this, and it had not
bothered him a bit after the first. It seemed to
be the right thing for her to do, or it might be
that most things she did seemed to be right.
P t this time he did not like it.

"'ll have to be goin'," he announced, abruptly.

"es, it is growing late," assented Mrs. Shel-
approaching the bed.

"He will come for good-bye to-morrow," said
Gracie.

"Can't do it, nohow," the Baby protested.
"Can't get off work till evening."

"Then you must bid her good-bye now."

"Yes, I will." But he paused a considerable
while, and then added, "What 'll I say to her?"

The child laughed playfully, and the mother,
not understanding his indecision, said: "Anything you choose—'Good-bye, Gracie.'"

He looked up at her in hesitation and perplex-
ity. "Kin I call her Gracie?" he asked.

"Certainly you may."

"That's my name, Robin," said Gracie, with
good-humored gayety.

"'GOOD-BYE, GRACIE,' HE REPEATED"

Mrs. Sheldon was struck by a sudden swift change that came over his countenance. For a single moment all the precocious hardness melted away, and the expression he wore offered no contradiction to the beauty of his features.

"Good-bye, *Gracie*," he repeated. The words were indistinctly uttered, and Mrs. Sheldon had another cause for surprise in what she took to be his unprecedented diffidence. Whatever the feeling was, it created within him an effect so peculiar and disagreeable that he lost no time in getting out of the room. Nothing exasperated him more than the puzzling sensations which occasionally came over him when he was in communication with or thinking about the "Sheldon kid."

His spirits were brightened before he left the house by the present of a five-dollar note from the head of the establishment, "for trying to behave himself and giving Gracie something to talk about." This was intended by Mr. Sheldon as a token of final dismissal. He did not approve of certain plans which his wife had partly formed for the future, and deemed it advisable to let the "little freak" sink back to his normal obscurity during the absence of the family from town.

"You never can make anything that isn't

crooked out of that sort of trash," he affirmed. "Give him a good send-off, and let him scamper away out of sight and mind. That will be best all around."

VII

FOUR hours later the Baby stole into the silent street upon which the Sheldon house was situated, and reconnoitred. The night was well suited to his purpose; heavy clouds were in the sky, and there was no meddlesome moonlight to be feared. He did not think it necessary to take extraordinary precautions, for he had been in the habit latterly of roaming through the district at all hours, and he knew how deserted it was sure to be in the early morning.

"Never catch a cop on this beat after dark," he said to himself; "it's too genteel."

He pushed back the iron gate slowly, to prevent it from creaking, and wedged a stone beneath it so that it should not close by itself. Then he crept stealthily across the garden, avoiding the gravel-walk and stepping only on the grass, until he stood under the window to which he proposed to climb. The blinds were shut; but he had no doubt that he could push them aside, and he knew he should find no other obstacle to his admission.

He had brought with him a fishing rod and line of the simple pattern with which boys of his class occasionally waste their time on the city piers. Leaning this against the trellis, he started upward, taking the greatest pains to keep from rustling the vines or shaking the wood-work. He had no difficulty in making his way aloft. His shoes had been left at home, and he planted his bare feet on the crossbars as noiselessly and securely as if he were endowed with the acrobatic instincts of a chimpanzee.

"Couldn't have been better," he chuckled, " if they'd ha' built it for me o' purpose."

When he had gone as high as the length of his fishing-rod he stopped and wound a loop of the line around his neck, and then proceeded, carrying his odd implement in this manner. The window was about twenty feet from the ground. On reaching it he turned about and examined the space below.

"I kin risk a jump," he reflected, " if old Sheldon wakes up and drives me hard. He won't shoot. They're all too soft for that here."

He did not at first unfasten the blinds, but merely moved a slat in its socket, and peered through the crevice. A lamp was dimly burning at the bedside, and by its light he could see everything within with sufficient distinctness. Gracie was alone, sleeping peacefully, her sweet and innocent face turned directly towards him. He looked at her steadily for some minutes— much longer than he was aware of—before giving attention to any other object. It would have satisfied him better if she were not so plainly visible. Casting his eyes about, he perceived that the door through which he had been accustomed to enter was wide open. He remembered the passage beyond it, and understood that the parents must be in the opposite chamber. The heavy breathing of a man warned him, in fact, that Mr. Sheldon was dangerously near. But there was little to be alarmed at in this circumstance. It was a good thing, on the contrary, to be thus assured that the head of the household was not awake. A door on the other side of the room was closed, and it was not likely that any interruption would come from that direction.

Preparations for the journey of the following day had evidently been prolonged to a late hour. Many articles were removed from the toilet-stand, and the contents of a chest of drawers had been taken out and placed near a trunk. But the jewels which he had longed to possess himself of were lying precisely where he had seen them, and were almost within his grasp as he stood clinging to the window-sill. Not only these shone in plain view, but he also saw glimmering in a velvet-lined box, on the top of the chest of drawers, a cluster of gems which he rightfully judged to be of much greater value than the trinkets with which he was familiar. Was it possible that he could likewise get these into his clutches? Such good-luck was almost too much to hope for. He would not, at any rate, consider the matter until he had gathered in the more accessible plunder.

He now swung the blinds gently, stirring them but a fraction of an inch at a time, to make sure that the hinges should not grate. When they were out of his way, and the whole breadth of the window was clear, he pulled up the fishing-rod and hung a large hook at the end, upon a piece of line some six inches in length. This he cautiously pushed into the chamber until it hovered over the toilet-stand, about five feet in advance of him. The first object he fished for was a slender gold bracelet. He had considerable difficulty in getting the point of the hook under its edge, but after this was accomplished it was a simple business to lift the prize over to his reach, to disengage it, and drop it into his pocket. One after another he secured in the same way a

second golden bracelet, a watch-chain, and a
small breastpin in the shape of a cross. He was
drawing this last towards him when his wander-
ing glance fell upon Gracie. He stopped short,
and an indescribable thrill ran through him—
another of the queer disturbances to which he
had latterly been subject; disturbances hitherto
foreign to his experience, and all the more un-
welcome from his inability to resist or explain
them.

"These gimcracks don't belong to *her*, anyway," he meditated. "They're worth too much,
and they're too big—all except this one. I might
shove this one back."

But the impulse had barely shaped itself in
his mind when he stifled it in angry disgust at
his folly. Was he losing his wits? He felt himself turning red with shame. He might as well
be a baby in earnest if his backbone was worth
no more than this to him.

He deposited the little breastpin with the rest
of the spoil, and went on hauling in a few less
costly trifles, with an occasional hungry look at
the more substantial and tempting assortment in
the far-away corner. There was the making of
him in that pile, he calculated. One ring alone,
if its gleam could be trusted, was equal to a
fortune, and there were at least half a dozen

strung together, of various qualities. What were his chances of getting at them? It could do no harm to think them over, whether any result came or not.

Presently he detached the hook and cord which he had thus far put to such profitable use, and taking a lump of soft putty from a pocket in his shirt, moulded it into a ball on the tip of his pole. If he could only cover the distance to the top of the chest of drawers, and make a dab at two or three of the precious stones, the game might be played safely enough. But a single trial showed that the stretch was too great. It was distracting. Why had he not brought a proper pole, instead of a toothpick like this? He wondered if there was time to go in search of another. No, that was out of the question. Yet to give up such a splendid mass of booty, when nothing stood between it and him but a half-dozen yards of empty air, was enough to drive him to frenzy.

As he gazed ravenously, the blood seemed to run like liquid fire through his veins, and a feeling of blind desperation took control of him. Come what might, he would not leave without an effort to make those treasures his own. It was worth risking his liberty or his limbs, and almost his life. A fury of greed was upon him. He lowered the fishing-rod to the ground outside, and in an instant slipped through the window, alighting noiselessly on the floor. The thick carpet deadened his footsteps, and enabled him to walk without a sound to the open door. Closing this with a deftness of touch that showed he had not thrown aside the methods of prudence in the madness of his rash resolve, he turned the key, and sprang behind a large arm-chair for concealment in case the lock should snap so loudly as to awaken the sleeping girl. But the click was scarcely audible, and she did not stir.

Watching her narrowly, he swiftly crept around the bed and stood facing the box which contained the brilliants. The collection was not so magnificent as he believed, but it was dazzling enough to have set the covetous instincts of a much more mature thief glowing at white-heat. It made him giddy to have them so near his eyes. And they were all his, or would be in less than five minutes. Should he take box and all, or transfer the contents to his pockets? The box, by all means. It was heavy, but he could get it down into the garden without much effort, and empty it there, comparatively at his leisure.

Thus deciding, he lifted it with both hands, and started to return to the window.

"IN AN INSTANT HE SLIPPED THROUGH THE WINDOW"

VIII

" Are you looking at my bangles, Robin?"

The voice was gentle and subdued, as he had always heard it, and the words came in a drowsy little murmur, but a thunder-clap could not have fallen upon the Baby's ear with a sharper shock. He staggered as he set the box down, and the room seemed whirling around before his eyes; but even in that moment of terror and confusion his cunning did not desert him.

"Hush! hush!" he said, in a tremulous whisper, running hastily to the bedside. "Don't speak so loud. Yer mother's fast asleep."

" Oh yes; then she left you to take care of me, I suppose."

"Talk soft, I tell yer. She's all tired out. I'm a-lookin' after yer while she rests."

"Poor mamma! I'll be ever so careful. Did you come to say good-bye again?"

" Yes, yes; that's what I come for."

"I'm glad I waked up. Thank you, Robin; you are always a good boy. Do you like to see my bangles?"

" Them things? I seen 'em just now."

"Please bring them here; I will show you."

The boy obeyed her mechanically, keeping a close watch upon the door he had locked, and with every muscle ready for a dash to the window at the slightest sound from another part of the house.

"But these are not mine; these are mamma's. Turn up the light, Robin; see how beautiful they are. My bangles are smooth and plain. Won't you look for them?"

Her bangles! Then the things now in his pockets did belong to her—some of them at least. He stared at her wildly and half dazed.

"Where'll I find 'em?" he said, huskily.

"What makes you speak so strange, Robin?"

"So's not to make a noise. Hush!"

"Oh, but you look strange, too; your forehead is all wet."

"It's nothin'. Lemme get your things."

He went to the table, and while pretending to make a search, contrived to remove the ornaments from his pockets without being observed by Gracie.

"These what yer want?" he asked, returning.

"Yes, these are mine." She lifted the little breastpin and held it out to him. "See, Robin, this was for you."

"What d'yer mean?" he said, taking it from her with a shaking hand.

"One evening, after you went away, I made mamma promise me—if I should die—to give it to you for a keepsake."

"No, yer didn't! Yer didn't do it; don't yer tell me that!" The poor wretch dropped the cross upon the floor and hid his face, now haggard and distorted with pain.

"What's the matter, Robin? I didn't die; I'm well again, you see. You mustn't cry."

"I ain't a-cryin'. I never cried in my life. It's hot here; I'm goin' away. Gi' me them shiners; I'll put 'em back; I'll put 'em all back."

He did this hurriedly, and then picked up the pin he had let fall, and laid it on the bed.

"You may keep that, Robin," said the child. "I know mamma will let me give it to you. I want you to have it, because you felt so sorry just now."

The boy caught at his throat and breast as if he were suffocating. Never had he felt a pang like that which now shot through him.

"D'yer want—to drag out—my heart—and stamp on it?" he gasped. "No, no," he added, with a sudden change of manner; "don't be frightened. I wouldn't frighten yer for the whole

world—*Gracie*. I'm sick, that's all. I'm not fit
to be here."

"Poor Robin, how white you are! No, I
never am frightened. But if you are sick I will
call mamma."

"No, no," he stammered; "I'll be right as
soon as I get out. Don't say a word. Keep still
just a minute more."

"But you must take the cross to remember me
by."

"I can't do it; wish I could, but I can't. If
you had some cheap thing to give me—"

"This is cheap enough, you silly boy. I *want*
you to have it."

"Then I will, and thank yer. And I'll say
good-bye—the last time."

"Till I come home again," she answered, cheerfully.

"The last time; the last time!"

He sprang to the window, and had one foot
over the edge before she guessed his intention.
Startled at the unexpected action, she raised herself on her elbow and called out loudly: "What
are you doing, Robin? You'll kill yourself!"

He whirled about, and lifted his arm with a
gesture of entreaty. As he did this the trinket
slipped from his fingers and fell upon the carpet.
At the same moment a rush was heard in the

passage, and a heavy blow was struck against the door. His head began to spin, but though dizzy with excitement he still had no fear of capture, for the door was locked, and he knew he could reach the garden with a bound. Even at this desperate crisis he had other thoughts than those of escape.

"I can't go without it!" he exclaimed, darting back and stooping for the cross. He found it in an instant, but before he could fling himself outside of the window, the child, roused to an activity of which he could not have believed her capable, leaped from the bed and seized him by the arm.

"You are crazy, Robin!" she screamed.

"Lemme jump!" he cried, hoarsely, struggling, though not with violence, to release himself. "Yer'll be the death of me!"

While the words were on his lips, the door at the extremity of the room, which he had not thought it necessary to secure, was thrown open, and in a flash Mr. Sheldon was upon him, gripping his neck fiercely. A second later the boy was sprawling on the floor and the enraged father glaring down at him with flaming eyes.

"Oh, papa, take care; it's Robin," pleaded Gracie, crying piteously in her agitation and affright.

"Get back to bed, dear," Mr. Sheldon replied;
"I have him safe."

"Yes, yer've got me," sneered the Baby, "and
how did yer get me? Yer don't s'pose *she* could
ha' held me if—"

"If what, you ruffian?"

"If I hadn't been afraid o' hurtin' her?"

"Gracie, are you hurt?" her father hastily exclaimed.

"Why, no, papa; it's Robin!"

"Yes, yes; go to your bed."

Mr. Sheldon was on the point of calling for his
wife, when that lady entered, in great alarm.

"This brute has broken into the house," said
the husband, pointing to the Baby, who had now
risen. "And see; what's this he has in his
hand? Gracie's gold cross--the thief!"

"I gave it to him, papa. He didn't want to
take it, but I made him."

"Indeed! Then where—" Mr. Sheldon glanced
around the room, and, to his amazement, saw that
although the other valuables had been somewhat
disarranged, they were all apparently in or near
the places where they had been left.

"Why did you come here?" said Mrs. Sheldon
to the Baby, more sternly than he had ever
heard her speak.

Loyal little Gracie would not leave her protégé

"'OH, PAPA, TAKE CARE; IT'S ROBIN,' PLEADED GRACIE"

undefended. "He came to bid me good-bye again," she declared, with great animation, sitting upright in her bed.

"Hush, my daughter!" her mother commanded. folding the grieved little creature in her arms. "Say nothing unless you are asked."

"But you don't understand, mamma," Gracie remonstrated, too eager and anxious to yield the accustomed submission. "He has been here ever so long. I showed him all your ornaments, and we talked about everything."

"How did he get here?"

"I don't know; he told me—" Gracie checked herself, recalling the deception of the lad's first speeches.

"Well?"

"He told me a story, I'm afraid," the girl confessed, hanging her head.

"You may be sure he did," cried her father. "The fellow is all lies. You came in by the window, you impudent vagabond. What was it for?"

"You heard what she said," replied the Baby, stolidly. and hunching his shoulders.

"I heard that, but I want to know the truth."

"George, if it *should* be the truth," said Mrs. Sheldon. appealingly, as the culprit remained silent. It did not strike the devoted mother as so

11

very unnatural that a rude outcast of immature
years should have become romantically attached
to her child, or that his adoration should mani-
fest itself in fantastic escapades.

"Nonsense, Helena! How can you say such
things? Do you imagine a fellow like this can
be moved by the feelings which you attribute to
him? There! let us end the matter. Look to
Gracie, and I will question him in our room.
Are the servants astir?"

"I think not."

"Very good; they are not to be called until I
have need of one of them."

Ordering the Baby to follow him, he went to
his own chamber. This time Gracie made no
protest. She was sad and bewildered. The discovery that her Robin had been guilty of false-
hood was a stroke that shattered her simple faith
in him.

"Papa will do what is right," said her mother,
striving to soothe her. "You know he never
wishes to be harsh or unforgiving." But she
felt that the boy had forfeited every claim to
forbearance, and had little hope that her husband would be mercifully inclined towards one
who had so shamefully abused her kindness and
trust.

IX

Mr. Sheldon paced the floor, thinking rapidly. The case certainly presented strange features. He had seen for himself that the boy need not have been caught if he had chosen to exert his strength in repulsing the little girl. He had stood almost passive while her arms were wound about him. That was to be noted in his favor. As to the jewels, he had handled them all, and made no attempt to carry a single one away, except the trifle which Gracie insisted she had forced upon him. Yet why should he be in the house at all? It was a most mysterious business; but the more he reflected upon it, the less he was inclined to press an investigation. It would compel him to defer his visit to the country, and bring upon him and his family a notoriety not at all to his taste. He particularly dreaded the ridicule which, he foresaw, would attach to his wife for the injudicious confidence she had lavished upon this young house-breaker.

After deliberating perhaps five minutes, he stopped walking, and announced his decision thus:

"I don't see why I should waste time over a vagabond of your pattern. It will be more trouble to me to have you arrested than to let you run clear. You can go—though it is better luck than you deserve—and a good riddance to you."

The Baby did not stir. He too seemed to have something to turn over in his mind. He waited so long that Mr. Sheldon sharply bade him bestir himself and leave. The only response was a most unexpected inquiry:

"Am I to go for good?"

"Good or bad, I don't care. What do you mean?"

"I mean, will yer ever let me come here again?"

Mr. Sheldon laughed in mockery at this daring flight of audacity. "You have cheek enough for a regiment of burglars," he said.

"So I sha'n't never speak to her after this?"

"Who—my daughter? Not if I can help it. Come along, and make haste."

"Then I won't go," said the boy, stubbornly.

"You won't? We shall see about that!" exclaimed Mr. Sheldon, beginning to lose his temper at this crowning exhibition of insolence.

"I don't go out of the house no such a way as this. I'll stay where I am till I'm run in, and then I'll take my term in Sing Sing. That's what's the matter with me, and yer may make what yer please of it!"

The Baby's intention was so energetically stated, and with such intensity of emphasis, that Mr. Sheldon more than half suspected he was dealing with a lunatic; but he was not left long in this misconception.

"Yer kin send for a cop, and I'll blow the whole trick. I came here to lift them di'monds and things — just that an' nothin' else. I had half of 'em stowed in my pocket one time. I'm a thief, that's what I am. Now bring along yer police an' yer handcuffs; I'm ready!"

Here was a real surprise. The rascal was in earnest; there could be no question about that. He looked his captor full in the face, which he had not done before, and there was a glitter in his eye which betokened spirit at least, and dogged resolution.

"Why do you tell me this?" inquired the astonished gentleman.

"'Cause yer say I sha'n't see her no more."

"Do you think you are fit to see her?"

Mr. Sheldon was vexed with himself as soon as he put this interrogation. What business had he to be parleying with the cub? The proper course was to get him out of the way as quickly

as possible. But he had asked the question, and
would hear the answer.

"I *ain't* fit to see her; I know that well enough
—*but I want to.*"

The Baby's face was ghastly to look at after
he had uttered these words. His teeth were set
fast, the muscles of his mouth were contracted,
and his forehead was twisted and wrinkled with
the effort he made to hold himself in restraint.
Tears gathered in his eyes—not such tears as
are shed on light provocation of boyish grief or
shame, but tears that were wrung from him by
an anguish the like of which he had never known
before, and which he was as unable to comprehend as to control. They scalded him as they
fell upon his cheeks, but he made no attempt to
wipe them away, and kept his lids wide apart,
staring straight before him. He felt that it was
a degrading weakness for one of his stamp to
cry like a sick girl, but he would not add to it
the greater weakness of concealment. Since his
treacherous nerves had given way and allowed
all his pluck to forsake him, he could certainly
gain nothing by setting up a ridiculous pretence
of fortitude.

Mr. Sheldon was a practical man of the world,
and if anybody had related to him the incidents
in which he was now taking part he would have

laughed at the notion that the lad could be sincere. But the evidence of his own senses could not be resisted. The suffering was genuine, whatever the cause, and he was not so hard or severe a man as to be able to witness it without a shade of pity. Was it indeed conceivable that the unconscious influence of a little child had brought this untamed animal to such a degree of subjugation? He had heard of similar occurrences, particularly in romances and on the stage, but had never considered them entitled to much credit. Yet who should presume to limit the possibilities of human nature, or determine by what hidden impulses the mind could be swayed for good or evil? If the boy were not deceiving himself, as well as trying to deceive others, he might be on the verge of a transformation through which the plan of his whole life could be reshaped. Had he, the prosperous and fortunate citizen, the right to crush out this chance that was perhaps struggling to assert itself for the regeneration of a vagabond and criminal?

He had not often been called upon to consider his moral obligations towards people of a lower social station than his own, and he was by no means pleased with the position in which he now found himself placed. But it was not his habit to shirk responsibilities when he once realized that they rested upon him, and after pondering a while he came to a conclusion which he thought just and reasonable, and which alone, he believed, could lead to satisfactory results.

"Listen to me," he said, putting himself face to face with the self-avowed thief: "This may be a more serious moment than you suppose, and you will do well to drop all nonsense and take a long look ahead. You are free to go now and choose your own road for one year. I don't want to see you or hear from you in that time. If you can come at the end of it, and prove that you have led a decent life, and are endeavoring to make a man of yourself, I'll befriend you— and so shall my little girl, if she likes. I sha'n't give you a penny to start with. If you're not a fool, you'll know why; if you are a fool, it doesn't matter, for then you'll not come back anyway. That is all I have to say. As to the future, it depends entirely upon what show you can make one year from now."

The Baby drew a long breath. "I'll do it," he said, sturdily. "To-day's the first of August, eighteen eighty-nine. Yer'll see me on the first of August, eighteen ninety. I sha'n't give yer no trouble till then. There's—there's just one thing yer might do for me before I go. I know

"SENT HIM FORTH INTO THE DARKNESS"

I ain't got no right to ask it, but yer might be willing."

"You can't speak again this night to anybody here," replied Mr. Sheldon, stiffly.

"Course not. I didn't go to think o' that. What I meant was, perhaps yer'd let me take the pin she gave me — the bit of a cross. It'd do me a heap o' good if yer could. But if yer don't—"

"Well, if I don't?"

"No matter, then; it's all right. Perhaps she'll keep it for me till next year. Will yer—will yer tell her I spoke of it?"

"You shall have it now."

Mr. Sheldon then brought the little clasp, and having handed it to its new owner, led him down-stairs, and sent him forth into the darkness.

"A black night for the poor beggar," said the man of ease and prosperity, as the Baby disappeared in the gloom. "Will he ever get a glimpse of daylight, I wonder?"

X

EARLY the next morning a soiled envelope was found in the hall, with Mr. Sheldon's name pencilled upon it in large and uneven letters. It had been thrust under the front door, and it contained a five-dollar note, which was immediately recognized as the one given by the master of the house to the Baby on the previous evening.

The Sheldons went to the country, and remained two months. Shortly after their return another envelope, cleaner and more carefully addressed, was left in the same way for Gracie's mother. Three dollars in notes were enclosed, and a scrap of paper, on which was written, "Six halves -- $3."

There was no doubt where the money came from, nor why it was sent. Mrs. Sheldon was much gratified, and her husband began to hope the lad was working out his fortune in the right way. Nothing was said upon the subject to their child, whose recollection of the night of adventure grew dim as the months rolled by.

Summer came again, and as the end of July

drew near Mrs. Sheldon frequently spoke of the singular appointment, and discussed the prospect of the Baby's reappearance.

"I shall be sadly grieved if he does not come," she said.

"I shall be disappointed, too," Mr. Sheldon acknowledged. "It is the only fairy story I ever was mixed up in, and if our fairy stories can't end as we want them to, what is the use of having any?"

"Why do you call it a fairy story?" asked the lady.

"Blind mother, where are the eyes of your imagination?" laughed her husband, as he pointed towards Gracie, who sat in the same room, but out of hearing. "Can you look at the guiding spirit of it and repeat that question?"

They were sojourning at a watering-place during the holiday season; but Mr. Sheldon was so much interested in the result of his experiment that he willingly made arrangements to bring the family to town for a week, and the 1st of August found them temporarily at home. The morning and afternoon of that day passed without any sign from the Baby; but this was to be expected, as Mrs. Sheldon was reminded when she began to show indications of uneasiness. And in the evening, sure enough, there came a ring at the street door, and a letter was presently brought in by a domestic, with this request:

"The messenger asks you to let him stay in the hall, sir, till you finish reading it."

Mrs. Sheldon was for having him introduced and her daughter sent for at once, but Mr. Sheldon checked her, saying that the boy's suggestion was a sensible one, and had best be adhered to. He opened the missive, and read aloud, as follows:

> "THE ENTERPRISE BANK-NOTE Co.,
> NEW YORK, *August* 1, 1890.

"*Mr. George Sheldon:*

"DEAR SIR, — My youngest employé, Robin Grace, has requested me to send you an exact and unprejudiced statement as to his character for honesty and uprightness. It is with unusual satisfaction that I accede to his wish.

"He entered our establishment eight months ago in the humblest capacity, application having been made on his behalf by a society whose recommendation was sufficient to insure his admission. I was informed that he sought employment here, knowing that our subordinate attachés are necessarily subject to the strictest surveillance, on account of the responsible nature of the business, and desiring especially to make for himself a record under the most rigorous conditions that could be imposed.

"I have never been made acquainted with his purpose, but it gives me pleasure to certify that throughout his term of service his conduct has been above reproach. I should be glad to speak of the intelligence he has shown in the discharge of his duties, and the general propriety of his demeanor, but he begs me to confine my testimony to the single question of his integrity, and in that particular his reputation is unblemished.

"If it is your intention to withdraw him from our office, he will carry with him the regard and the best wishes of his employers. If your arrangements permit him to remain, I can promise him the promotion of which he has proved himself worthy.

"I am, sir, yours very truly,

"C. C. ALEXANDER."

It was a charm to see the light in Mrs. Sheldon's eyes as she listened to these words of warm approval. Her heart was filled with the content of a good woman who rejoices at the fulfilment of her generous hope for a fellow-being's rescue from degradation. She rose hastily, and left the drawing-room by a side door, saying, "I will send Gracie to bring him to us."

A minute later the little girl's feet were heard tripping through the hall. "Somebody for me?" she asked. "Come this way, please."

She entered from the obscurity, followed by a fine-looking lad of thirteen, neatly dressed in a dark blue knickerbocker suit, whose countenance shone with eager expectation. Mr. Sheldon would not have known him. Even his wife, who had hastened back to witness the reception, was unprepared for so thorough a change. There were the same striking features, and the clear, delicate complexion, but the uncouth wildness was gone, and the ungoverned restlessness had given place to a quiet and respectful bearing. He was the picture of a little gentleman as he stood in the doorway awaiting recognition.

"Why, it's my Robin!" cried Gracie, springing towards him with delight. "I always told you he was a nice boy. What do you think now, mamma?"

He had no reason to complain of his greeting, and a few minutes after the first salutation he was sitting at his ease and chatting as freely as Gracie's impetuous interruptions would allow.

"How handsome you have grown!" she suddenly exclaimed. "Are you not glad?"

"I'm glad if you are satisfied with me," he

answered, very much flushed. Possibly he was not yet completely reconciled to the refinement and attractiveness of his personal appearance.

"I see your employer gives you your full name," Mrs. Sheldon remarked. "Have you found your parents?"

"No, ma'am," said the boy, turning still redder. "I thought — you know your little girl called me by one name — the only one anybody ever gave me in a friendly way—and of course I kept that. But I had to have another when I —when I—you know what I mean, sir—and I thought perhaps you wouldn't mind if I owed her the second one, too. But I can change it if you don't like."

"I see," responded Mr. Sheldon; "Robin Grace; very neat and very well thought of. Gracie, this young man is your godson; do you know that? He is doubly your godson, for you have had the naming of him twice over."

Gracie did not understand at first, but when it was explained to her she vowed that nothing could be more to her fancy.

"Did you really, Robin, name yourself after me? How good that is! I didn't know you *could* do such a thing."

"I hadn't any that really belonged to me—not

that I ever heard of—and there's no name I—
not any that I think so much of. So if your
father and mother are willing—"

"Keep it, my boy, keep it," said Mr. Sheldon;
"and I hope it will bring you good." He intended to say more, but a curious tingling in his
nose, such as gentlemen of mature years do not
like to have come upon them unawares, prevented him from continuing. Mrs. Sheldon, being a
woman, did not care so much about preserving
an undisturbed composure, and could let her
voice quaver without feeling humiliated. So she
kept up the conversation until her husband had
taken care of the cold in his head of which he
suddenly became aware.

"Well, Robin," he said at length, "we have a
great many matters to settle in course of time,
but the most important question is, who is to
take care of you? Shall it be Mrs. Sheldon, or
I, or Gracie? Gracie has the first right, I admit; but perhaps she isn't quite equal to it just
at present."

"Oh, sir," replied the lad, overflowing with
happiness, "I think I sha'n't have much difficulty in taking care of myself in one way, but if
anybody is to take care of me in the other way
—the way you mean—the best way—I hope it
may be your little daughter. She did something

for me a year ago that nobody else could have done. I didn't see how it was then, but I know better now; and I guess there's no other person that can look after me so well for a good many years to come."

"Robin, Robin, what funny things you say!" cried Gracie, to whose bright young mind these graver thoughts were not attuned.

"Oh yes," he persisted; "I sha'n't willingly have anybody but you for a guardian; but in case it gets too much for you sometimes, perhaps your father and mother will help you a little."

"There's not much fear of that, my lad. Unless I am more mistaken than I ever was in my life, the day is not likely to come when you will turn to either of us in vain, or when we shall be made to feel that we have misplaced our interest and confidence in Gracie's godson."

12

NATTY BARTON'S MAGIC

I

In the very front row of seats in Fenlowe Hall sat Natty Barton, eagerly waiting for the wonders to begin. He thought he had never before been so happy. Fenlowe was a small country town, and, so far as he could recollect, this was the first real magician that had ever come there. It was the first public entertainment of any sort that he had attended, although he was fully twelve years old. He was too poor to have money for such pleasant purposes. But by a happy chance, quite as marvellous, Natty believed, as anything he was about to witness, he had been standing in front of the exhibition building that afternoon just when the conjurer needed help in arranging his materials on the stage. Natty was called in from the street, and, being found quick and willing, was rewarded with a ticket for the evening's performance. He had no difficulty in getting permission to be present, and now, dressed for the occasion in his best clothes, he awaited the wizard's appearance in a glow of delightful expectation.

Presently the wonder-worker walked upon the platform, leading a little girl about ten years of age, who, Natty said to himself, was the prettiest child he had ever beheld. The audience seemed to be of the same opinion, and the loud applause was evidently intended more as a greeting to her than to her companion. But the conjurer had no reason to be dissatisfied with his reception as soon as he began to unfold the mysteries in store. To the populace of Fenlowe his exploits were bewildering. Natty was lost in amazement. Up to that point of his life he had thought his eyes could be trusted, but now they were capable of nothing but playing him tricks. Such funny tricks, too, that his face ached with the fits of laughter into which he was thrown. When the magician strolled up to old Mullins, the lessee of the hall, and pulled a live rabbit out of his waist-coat-pocket, the people shrieked with glee, and Natty nearly fell off his seat. But the cross-tempered lessee did not like it so well. He muttered something disagreeable, whereat the magician instantly drew a big goose from the back of his neck, saying, with a roguish smile,

"Why, sir, do you carry your family about
with you in this way?"

Mullins looked very savage, but he was disliked
by the whole town, and nobody cared except his
son, Ned Mullins, who was sitting near Natty, and
who glared about him with as fierce an air as a
boy of fourteen could put on. The performer
was somewhat disturbed by the old man's resent-
ment. Turning towards him, he said, pleasantly:

"No offence, I hope, sir. My little girl shall
make it up to you when the sweetmeats are
passed around."

"Perhaps I'll make it up to *you*, my man, before the night is out," growled old Mullins.
Then the people hissed at him, and young Mullins grew red as a lobster, and twice as ugly.

The magician soon went back to his place, and
announced that he was about to attempt an exceedingly difficult trick, in which he desired the
assistance of one or two young gentlemen from
the audience, if they would favor him by coming
upon the stage. Natty felt himself tingling all
over. He would have given worlds to go and
stand near that bewitching little lady, but he did
not dare. He was not sure that the term "young
gentleman" was meant for a boy like him. To
his astonishment, however, Ned Mullins left his
seat and clambered up to the platform without

the least sign of embarrassment. Natty thought he was as much of a young gentleman as Ned Mullins any day; but still he did not stir, although he half fancied that he saw a shade of disappointment in the pretty girl's countenance.

"Another, please," said the magician; and as he spoke he glanced right down into Natty's eyes. This was as good as a direct invitation; so Natty, very much agitated, hastened to respond. He was as red as Ned Mullins when he reached the stage, but not so ugly, by many degrees. The little girl nodded to him, and that made him more comfortable, for he was sure she had not done anything of the kind when Ned Mullins approached her.

The necromancer began his feat by handing a leaden bullet to Natty, and asking him to carry it down among the spectators, so that some one could make a secret mark upon it with a knife. Then he took a large pistol from a table, and held it while Natty, under instructions, put in a lot of powder, and afterwards the ball, covering it all the while, so that the mark should not be detected by the performer. Every one saw that this was done fairly enough.

The magician next carried the pistol across to where Ned Mullins stood, and gave it into his hands, telling him to watch it carefully, and keep it in a particular position. Ned said he would do so, but as soon as the conjurer turned away, Natty observed that the other boy drew something swiftly from his pocket and passed his hand over the muzzle of the weapon. What to say or do Natty did not know, and before he could collect his thoughts the magician again came forward, followed by the child, who carried a great globe filled with goldfish. As she took her position in the middle of the stage, a dreadful chill came over Natty. He could not foresee what was to happen, but he was suddenly stricken with a fear that some calamity was at hand. Without exactly understanding why he did it, he ran towards the girl, exclaiming:

"Let me hold it, please. It is—it is too heavy for you."

The magician was surprised.

"Thank you, my young friend," he said; "you are very polite, but it is not so heavy as it seems, and Adela is used to it."

"I wish you would let me," pleaded Natty.

Once more the magician looked inquiringly at him, whereupon he lowered his voice and whispered:

"Don't—don't use the pistol, sir; Ned Mullins did something to it."

The magician started, but quickly recovered

himself, and, addressing the audience, said : " The young gentleman is more considerate than many of his years would be. There; no one need hold the vase; we will set it on the table."

Having done this, he walked across to Ned Mullins and relieved him of his charge. Natty was in dire apprehension until the magician returned and said, in a murmur, as he passed, " Be not alarmed, my good lad; all is safe."

A minute after, the pistol was pointed directly at the vase and fired at short range, without injuring the glass, although the fish began swimming about in wild disorder. Natty's anxiety was happily dispelled. Having read descriptions of a trick similar to this one, he had been terrified by the idea that the weapon was to be turned upon the little girl.

" Now Adela will carry the globe to the gentleman who marked the bullet," said the magician. " I do not wish to touch it at all."

The child obeyed the direction, and as she moved through the throng a large goldfish was seen dragging a heavy object attached by a cord to its tail. This was taken out, and pronounced to be the very ball on which the private mark had been cut.

In the midst of the applause which followed, the magician spoke thus to Natty: "Will you come to us at the hotel to-night after the performance? Do, if you can."

"Oh yes," answered Natty, highly elated. "I am sure mother will let me."

Turning to Ned Mullins, the magician added, in a severe tone: "I do not ask you to come, and you know the reason why. It would serve you well if I exposed you before the people. Leave the stage, and come near us no more!"

II

An hour later Natty was led by the magician, whose name was Ross, into a private parlor of the hotel, where he found Adela and her mother, a lady about thirty years of age, whose delicate appearance indicated that she was an invalid.

"My wife has been ailing for many weeks," said Mr. Ross; "but this fine country air will do her great good. We shall stay here till she is stronger."

"We hope to," the lady remarked.

"Mamma, we *must*," exclaimed Adela, "if it will help you."

"We must if we can," said Mr. Ross. "Sit down, Master Natty, and give me a little information, if you please. How many of our exhibitions do you think your townspeople will endure without getting tired of us?"

"How could they ever get tired?" cried Natty, impulsively. "I could go a hundred times."

"You are very complimentary," said the conjurer; "but if the hall can be filled seven or eight times we shall be satisfied. Perhaps my wife will be well enough to give some assistance towards the end. Then you shall have a performance worth seeing."

"Everything to-night was as beautiful as it could be," Natty declared.

"Except the pistol trick," said Mr. Ross, laughing. "That would have gone wrong but for your help."

"Did I really help?" asked Natty, vastly pleased. "I am so glad. I was afraid—"

"You were afraid I was going to shoot at Adela. Oh no, I never do that, although there would be no danger at all if nobody meddled with the pistol. Many conjurers do fire at people, but I dislike the practice. Do you know what that mischievous fellow did?"

"He would do anything bad," Natty replied. "He is the meanest boy in town."

"Of course you understand," said Mr. Ross, "as everybody does, that my wonderful exploits are simply ingenious deceptions. You need not tell your friends, but I have a way of taking out the bullet without appearing to. After I had done this, the young scamp dropped a couple of marbles into the pistol-barrel. It would have been very awkward if you had not warned me. The globe would have been broken, the fishes killed, and the entertainment spoiled. Our little girl might have been badly hurt by the broken glass, for she usually holds the vase. So you see we have good reason to thank you."

"Indeed we have," exclaimed Mrs. Ross, warmly. "Come and give me your hand, my dear boy."

"And let me have the other," said Adela, going quickly to him. "Papa did not tell me this before."

Natty had never felt prouder or more contented. He tried to say something in acknowledgment of these kind speeches and actions, but before he could think of the proper words a loud knock was heard, and Mr. Ross left the group to open the door.

"Ah, the lessee," he said. "Come in, sir."

"Not I," answered Mullins, roughly. "My business is short. You thought it mighty smart to make me ridiculous and get me hissed a while ago. I know a trick as good as any of yours, my fine fellow. You can't have my hall after this week."

"Mr. Mullins," said Ross, "I had no intention of hurting your feelings. Nobody takes offence at my harmless jests."

"Then I'm nobody," retorted Mullins, "for *I* take offence. You have the hall for two more shows—one evening and one afternoon. I have signed to that, but nothing beyond. Take your rubbish out before Saturday night. That's all I have to say."

"Let me tell you," said Ross, mildly, "why I wish to remain a few weeks. My wife has had a long fit of sickness, and she needs rest and pure air. Her illness has prevented many of our performances this season, and we have made very little money. We cannot afford to stay here unless I give a series of entertainments. That is the absolute truth. Yours is the only hall in the place, and if you close it against us, we must go away. I trust you will consider the position I am in, and accept my apology if I annoyed you."

"I'm thinking of the position *I* was in when you made a fool of me before the crowd," snarled Mullins. "Out you go at the end of the week, and the town will be well rid of you."

The angry old man stalked away, and the conjurer rejoined his family with a downcast face.

Tears were in little Adela's eyes, and Natty himself was ready to cry. He felt that he ought to leave, but could not go without expressing his indignation, and trying to assure his new friends that they had his sympathy in their unexpected trouble.

"Old Mullins is worse than his boy Ned," he cried. "Everybody hates and despises him. I wish I dared to tell Mr. Huntington about this."

"Who is Mr. Huntington?" asked Mrs. Ross, smiling at the lad's vehemence.

"He lives in the big house opposite the old church," Natty replied. "I guess he is the richest man in the town. He is a lawyer, but he doesn't do any law work now. Most persons are afraid of him, just as I am. I don't know why; he isn't cross a bit. My mother is his house-keeper, and I live there too with her; but he never talks much to me. Indeed, he never talks much to anybody. They say he can do whatever he pleases in Fenlowe, and I don't believe he would let old Mullins behave so if he knew."

"Never mind, my lad," said Mr. Ross. "Who can tell what will happen? We have still two performances to give, and they may be more profitable than we expect. Take these tickets; we shall look for you Wednesday night and Saturday afternoon."

"Yes, do come," cried Adela. "I want you ever so much. Come up and help us again if papa calls for anybody."

"I'd do anything to help you," vowed Natty —"anything in the world if I only knew how."

"You are a good boy," chirped Adela, "so I shall kiss you for good-night."

Natty went home in a very unsettled state of mind. He wished something would happen by which he could prove in a manly, grown-up way how much he liked the whole Ross family, and how determined he was to stand by them. A beginning might be made, he thought, by picking a healthy quarrel with Ned Mullins; but there were reasons why he could not immediately carry out that plan. Ned Mullins was inconveniently handy with his fists, and capable of playing such tricks of legerdemain with Natty's features as would make it disagreeable for their owner to occupy a front seat in Fenlowe Hall, and would prevent him from offering his humble service in any part of the expected performances. He concluded that he must trust to luck for the desired opportunity, and postpone the affair with young Mullins until after the retirement of the conjuring party from Fenlowe, when a black eye more or less would be of trifling consequence.

III

Two evenings later, as Natty was crossing the hall of the large house in which he lived, just before starting for the exhibition, he saw Mr. Huntington standing near the front door, examining the pockets of his coat, which hung on a rack.

"Will you do me a favor, Natty?" said the lawyer. "I have left a paper which I need on my office table. Please run across the street and get it. Take a lantern with you. The document is tied with blue tape and has a number on it — 111. You can't forget that — one, one, one. Give it to your mother, and tell her to bring it to me. Here is my key."

Natty hurried over to the little office, and had no difficulty in finding what he had been sent for. The number was plain enough—"111"— and he noticed the word "lease" on the back, and the names of Huntington and Mullins. He delivered the paper to his mother, according to instructions.

"Yes, I suppose this is what Mr. Mullins is waiting for," she said. "He is in the library now."

"Dear me!" exclaimed Natty, "I wish Mr. Huntington had nothing to do with that old sinner."

He made his way quickly to Fenlowe Hall, and entered just as the performance began. Adela recognized him as he went to his seat, and during the evening he had the unspeakable delight of being summoned once or twice to the platform to take part in some complicated piece of necromancy. The entertainment was cordially applauded throughout, and towards the end a great impression was produced by an exhibition of what was called "second-sight," in which Adela, standing blindfold on the stage, accurately described various objects which her father borrowed from strangers in the audience. He would take a watch, or a ring, or any article that was offered him, ask the girl questions about it, and she would invariably answer with as much exactness as if her eyes were uncovered and she held it in her own hand.

When this was concluded, Adela was sent forward to distribute the contents of a basket of candies, while the magician made a little speech. He told the people that he had hoped to offer them an extended series of entertainments, but could now have the pleasure of meeting them only once more, on Saturday afternoon, permission to occupy the hall after that date having been positively denied him. He added that those who had been present on Monday evening would need no explanation of Mr. Mullins's hostility. He (Mr. Ross) had frankly expressed his regret at having wounded the lessee's delicacy, but that sensitive gentleman had declined to be pacified.

Mullins was standing, as usual, at the back of the hall. He now marched down the aisle, and when he had reached the centre, said, with a malicious grin: "You are not wanted in this place because I believe you are a humbug and a fraud. But I won't be too hard on you or anybody. You shall have a chance." He threw open his overcoat, and after fumbling a few seconds, drew a folded paper from the inside pocket. "Look here, Mr. Juggler," he continued, "if you or your girl can tell the indorsement on this sheet, or give the number and the names, I'll make it easy for you. No, you sha'n't come near me, either of you. The paper goes straight into my pocket again. If you can do what I propose without looking at it, you may have the hall as often as you like. If not, that's the end of it."

Chuckling at the idea of inflicting annoyance and mortification, he thrust the document back into his coat, which he buttoned tight. Many

persons, clearly perceiving how absurd and un-
reasonable his demand was, looked angrily at
him, but Natty Barton was trembling with excitement. He had recognized the paper by the
blue tape with which it was bound. It was the
same lease which he had held in his hands two
hours before. He beckoned to Adela, who stood
quite near him, and pretended to pick some candies from her basket. Everybody was giving attention to Mr. Ross, and Natty could speak softly without fear of being overheard.

"I know all about that paper," he whispered ;
"I know everything that is on the outside. Go
tell your father—quick, quick! Let him blindfold me, and I will settle old Mullins."

Adela stared at him in amazement. "Are you
sure?" she asked. "It seems so strange!"

"Of course I am sure. Do you think I would
make a mistake about a thing like this? Don't
lose a minute. Go tell your father."

Adela mounted hastily to the platform, from
which Mr. Ross was again addressing the spectators.

"The worthy lessee," he remarked, "is pleased
to call me a humbug. The word is not politely
chosen, but I shall not find fault with it. In a
certain way it is my business to be a humbug, at
your service, ladies and gentlemen. But he says

13

also that I am a fraud. I protest against the un-
truthfulness of that epithet. I do not deceive
you by pretending to possess supernatural power.
I endeavor to amuse you by seeming to accomplish impossible things. As for Mr. Mullins's
proposal, he is well aware that I undertake no
miracles."

"That's your affair," retorted Mullins. "I
give you a chance; you can take it or not, as
you like."

The conjurer was about to respond, when his
daughter approached him and hastily repeated
what Natty had told her. Mr. Ross paused and
gazed searchingly at the boy, who sat immediately below, and whose eager and determined expression of face was abundantly calculated to in-
spire confidence. After an instant's hesitation,
the magician turned once more to the audience,
most of whom were deeply indignant at Mullins's
behavior.

"I do not think it is true," he said, "that the
lessee has any intention of giving me a chance,
as he asserts. But we will see what can be done.
This is a most unusual thing to attempt, and if
I fail, I shall throw myself on your forbearance.
I am sure you will not think any the worse of
me."

Loud applause followed this modest avowal,

"PRETENDED TO PICK SOME CANDIES FROM HER BASKET"

at the end of which Mr. Ross bowed, and proceeded with his speech.

"If I succeed at all, I mean to succeed in a way that will be more surprising than anything I have yet done. In this matter I will not rely upon my little daughter for aid. I will request some young gentleman who is known to you all to take her place."

The general feeling was warmly in Mr. Ross's favor, and nearly a score of lads of various ages started towards the platform, Natty among them. It surprised him that he was not particularly called upon. He was not familiar with the cunning practices by which conjurers are accustomed to magnify the importance of their exploits.

"Thanks to you all," said the magician, "but I need only one. I think," he added, with an air of doubt, as if his mind were not already made up—"I think—yes, I will choose the youngest among you. That will be best. How old are you, my young friend?" he inquired, turning to a lad who was evidently Natty's senior.

"Fourteen, sir," was the answer.

"Fourteen. And you?" demanded Mr. Ross, looking at Natty.

"A little over twelve," said Natty, much relieved. He was beginning to comprehend Mr. Ross's methods.

"Very good," said the conjurer; "come hither, if you please."

Natty ascended, and was seated in a chair, with his back to the spectators. Adela bound his eyes with a handkerchief, and he was left alone. In the body of the hall everybody was keenly interested, and some showed not a little anxiety as Ross stepped into the aisle and slowly advanced to the spot where old Mullins had planted himself.

" Keep back !" cried the ugly-tempered lessee. " I won't let you see the paper."

" I have no wish to see it," said the conjurer, coolly, "and it gives me no especial pleasure to be near you. But if I perform this feat at all, I must do it according to my own plan."

" All right," growled Mullins; " but you don't play any more low games on me."

There was a murmur of irritation at this, and several persons cried " Shame !" but the object of their reproach laughed coarsely, and told the magician to make haste and get through with his mummery.

Ross moved on until he stood within five or six feet of his opponent. Then, looking him full in the face, he called out to Natty,

" Are you ready, my boy ?"

" Quite ready, sir."

" Look into your mind. Can you recognize the paper which this individual has in his coat-pocket ?"

" I can, sir; it is tied with a blue string."

" Anybody could see that," said Mullins, scorn-fully, " when I held it up."

" Are there," continued Ross, without heeding the interruption, " any names on the back of the paper ?"

" Yes, sir; there are two."

" Can you read them ?"

" I can, sir; the first is Huntington."

Mullins gave a start of astonishment. He could hardly believe his ears.

" And the other ?" pursued the wizard.

" The other is Mul-lins," replied Natty, pro-nouncing it in such a prolonged and comical tone of contempt that a burst of laughter echoed through the hall.

Mullins's countenance was a sight to behold. He was an ignorant man, and the unexpected result of the experiment gave him a very queer feeling. But he pulled himself together, and muttered, " There's the number yet to be told."

" True," said Ross; " the number."

Then Natty thought he would do something on his own account, to make the trick more effective. He raised his right hand in the air,

and moved the forefinger up and down three
times.

"The number?" he repeated. "Wait one moment, please. I see three lines. It might be—
I don't say it *is*, yet—but it might be three."

"It isn't three," shouted Mullins. "Nothing
of the sort. You have failed. I knew you
would."

"I don't say it is three," Natty ran on, hastily.
"Just wait a bit." Again he moved his finger
up and down as before. "No, it is not three,
yet there are three lines. I see—I have it now;
it is one hundred and eleven."

No confirmation in words was needed from
Mullins. His face was black with rage as he
swung himself about fiercely and left the hall.
The gentlemen in the audience cheered till the
windows rattled, and the ladies shook their hand-
kerchiefs so that the lights flickered. Mr. Ross
thanked them heartily, and led Natty forward
to receive his share of the demonstration. Adela
was enthusiastic in her gratitude.

"You dear boy," she said, after the people had
dispersed; "how beautifully you managed it!
Didn't he, papa? It was just as if he had been
on the stage all his life. You puzzled me, sir,
with your 'three lines.' I did not know what
was coming. How delighted mamma will be!"

"HE MOVED HIS FINGER UP AND DOWN THREE TIMES"

"It was a capital performance," Mr. Ross assented. "You have helped me immensely, Master Natty. Will you go with us to the hotel? Not to-night? Then come to-morrow. My wife will be glad to add her thanks to ours. This is the second good turn you have done us, and I'm sure I don't know how to repay you."

IV

WHEN Natty went to make his call on the following day he found bad news awaiting him. Mullins had broken his pledge. He had just notified Mr. Ross that in consequence of information privately received, he had concluded that the exhibitions were dangerous, and that he was bound in duty to suppress them. The astonished conjurer demanded an explanation, and was told that Mullins's son had discovered the secret of the pistol trick, which was of a nature to imperil human life. Such risks, he declared, should not be permitted in Fenlowe Hall. Ross retorted that there never had been anything wrong with the pistol until that mischievous boy had meddled with it, and that if any mishap had ensued, it would have been due solely to the malicious prank of

Mullins junior. But the old man continued to rail, and held to his resolution to drive the unfortunate family out of town.

This was too much for Natty, who straightway announced his intention to acquaint Mr. Huntington with the facts, and seek his intercession. He did not precisely know what that gentleman would be able to do, but had a vague conviction that nobody could stand against so much dignity, importance, and wealth as were united in his mother's patron. He trotted home, and summoning all his courage, presented himself, not without anxious misgivings, at the door of the library, in which the lawyer passed most of his afternoons.

"Come in," said Mr. Huntington, in response to Natty's timid knock. He was not a very old man, and there was never any harshness in his manner, but his unchanging gravity and stateliness of demeanor always impressed Natty with a sense of awe. The lad did not believe that any person alive had seen Mr. Huntington smile. His face was careworn, and he seemed to take no satisfaction in anything—at least, not in anything that boys could understand. Yet his speech was not severe, and his actions were often kind. Only last Independence Day he had enriched Natty with a prodigious box of fireworks, the possession of which would have filled the youngster's heart with perfect rapture if he had not been compelled to promise that none of the crackers or bombs should be exploded near the house. This spoiled a great part of Natty's enjoyment, whose filial wish had been to enliven his affectionate mother's nerves with a series of first-class Fourth of July sensations.

After much hesitation and a great deal of stammering, he succeeded in telling his story. Mr. Huntington listened silently, and when the recital was ended, began to ask questions.

"You say that Mr. Mullins first refused because he was angry with the conjurer, and afterwards on the ground of danger to the public?"

"Yes, sir."

"But there was no danger apart from that which young Mullins might have caused?"

"No, sir; none."

"Your idea about the lease was timely and ingenious; but did it not occur to you that as you had seen the names and the number while you were on an errand for me, it might be improper to disclose them?"

"I did think of that, sir; but I said to myself, if old Mullins—Mr. Mullins, I mean—was willing to talk about them, it wouldn't be wrong for me to do so too."

"Very well; I do not blame you. Your motive was a good one. But by-and-by, perhaps after this Mr. Ross has gone away, I advise you to explain to your friends how the trick was performed, and why. You should not give any one the chance to say that you had deceived people, or even misled them, without a worthy purpose."

"I understand that, sir; and I told mother last night how it happened."

"That is right. And as to the hall, I will inquire into that matter. If you have made no mistake, and Mr. Mullins has no other reason for excluding Mr. Ross, I think we will set aside his objections."

"Oh, can you, sir?" cried Natty, overjoyed at the success of his pleading.

"Why, I suppose so. You know that Fenlowe Hall belongs to me."

"No, sir, I did not know it; but I am so glad. May I tell Adela—and her father?"

"Not yet. Let me see Mullins first. Why do you wish to tell them?"

"It will please them so much, sir. Mrs. Ross is sick, and they want to stay here till she gets well. They thought they would be driven away by old Mullins—by Mr. Mullins—but if they could know at once—"

"I see. Well, you may say that if Mr. Ross

can satisfy the owner of the hall, he may continue to occupy it. But you will not mention my name, and he must not speak to the lessee upon the subject. If these conditions are not observed, I shall not interfere. Is that all, Natty?"

"Thank you; yes, sir. But— Yes, sir; that is all."

"You speak as if there was something more. What is it?"

Natty looked down at the floor, then up at the ceiling, and then out of the window, greatly embarrassed.

"Go on, my boy. Have you any reason to be afraid of me?"

"No, sir; oh no! Perhaps — perhaps I am afraid without any reason. Good-afternoon, sir." And Natty started to run away.

"Wait," said Mr. Huntington. "I am very sorry you are afraid of me. I don't think there is any need. Oblige me by saying what was on your mind."

"It was nothing," Natty persisted.

"Exactly; then it is all the easier to tell. Out with it."

"Well, sir; only this: The little girl does not look very well, either, and I thought—if I might —just for a few minutes—the river garden is so

beautiful now—and the weather is not too cold
—but no matter; good-afternoon, sir."

"You need not go yet," said Mr. Huntington; and he looked at Natty so curiously and
so long that the lad began to be afraid he had
been guilty of some frightful act of presumption.
"You know," proceeded the lawyer, "that visitors rarely come here. I am not in the best of
health myself, and I prefer to be alone. But I
think you will not disturb me. Yes, you may
bring your young friend to-morrow. Let her
come about noon, and tell your mother that I
shall be pleased if she will prepare some luncheon
for you both. That is all now, I presume."

"Yes, indeed, sir," Natty replied, quite unable
to express his delight in formal words. "I hope
you will excuse me for being afraid. I wish I
wasn't. Sometimes I can't help it. I will try—
but I don't know."

"Do so," said Mr. Huntington, gently enough,
but still without a smile. "Good-day."

Natty flew to his mother, and delivered his
news so breathlessly and in such broken and dis-
connected sentences that the excellent house-
keeper was in great concern lest her child had
strayed out of his senses.

"It can't be!" she exclaimed, after he had
contrived to unburden himself. "A strange girl

to come here! How did you dare to propose it?"

"Is it wrong, mother?"

"Wrong? No, not wrong; but I should not have dreamt of such a thing. There has not been a child in the house except you for years and years. I thought there never would be. It is a great event, Natty, though you cannot understand my reason for saying so."

"Why is it that nobody comes here, mother, and that Mr. Huntington seems to have no friends? Did he never like to know people?"

"Ah, Natty, I cannot tell you the whole now. Mr. Huntington had a heavy grief a long time ago. It was soon after you were born. He had an only sister whom he loved devotedly; but she married against his wish, and they parted in anger. He never saw her again."

"Where is she?" asked Natty, much impressed by his mother's gravity.

"She died soon after. It was a great blow to her brother, though he was right about the marriage. Helen's husband was not a fit man for her to wed. But Mr. Huntington could not forgive himself for his severity to her, and he has suffered ever since. He tried to do something to repair a part of his fault, but failed; and that made him more gloomy than he otherwise would have been. You shall hear it all some time, Natty, and then, young as you are, you will be sorry for him. I am glad he has broken the habit of closing the house to everybody. Perhaps brighter days will follow."

V

Mr. Ross's first two performances had been given on Monday and Wednesday evenings. The third was to take place Saturday afternoon. It was on Friday, a little before one o'clock, that Adela sat beside Natty at Mrs. Barton's table, enjoying the appetizing luncheon which the house-keeper had provided for the occasion. Adela had been almost speechlessly happy while roaming through the fine grounds under Natty's guidance. She had lived mostly in cities, and had never before been brought into such delightful contact with trees and flowers. Her zealous escort had taken her out on the river in a big boat, and had shown her the barn, the orchard, the duck-pond, the hen-house, the pigsty, and all the glories of the place. She looked a little tired, but very beaming and contented, as she chatted confidentially about the unfamiliar charms of the country. Once in a while, however, a shade passed over her countenance, and she seemed ill at ease.

Mrs. Barton did not fail to observe these signs of discomposure, but she made no remark or inquiry. Suddenly, however, she left the dining-room and went to the library, where her employer was seated, as usual.

"I beg pardon for disturbing you, sir," she began, "but I feel that you ought to know something this little girl has said. She told Natty she didn't think it would be right to go away without thanking you for letting her come here. She is a very intelligent child. Are you willing to see her?"

"No, Mrs. Barton," Mr. Huntington answered, quietly. "I am glad she has had some diversion, but her thanks are due to you and Natty."

"She does not think so, sir; and I believe it will trouble her very much if she cannot speak to you. She says her mother would reprove her if she neglected it. And, to tell you the truth, she is a little beauty. I do want to bring her to you, just for a moment."

"You are asking a very uncommon thing," said Mr. Huntington. "If she supposes she must make an acknowledgment, she can surely do so through you."

"If you could see her, sir, you would not say that. It is uncommon, I know, but I do not often try to put you out of your way. Let it be a favor to me."

"You shall have your wish, Mrs. Barton," the lawyer said, slowly, and still somewhat reluctantly. "But the child need not come here. If she is at luncheon I will look in casually. That will be less ceremonious and more agreeable to me."

"As you please, sir; and I am obliged to you for consenting."

A few minutes later Mr. Huntington walked into the dining-room, much to the surprise of Natty, who knew his habits of seclusion. Adela, divining who it was, laid down her knife and fork and rose from her seat. Her face flushed brightly as she waited for the master of the house to speak, but he was silent. He glanced hastily and strangely at Mrs. Barton, and then fixed his gaze upon the young visitor with an intentness that deepened the color in her cheeks.

"What is your name, my little friend?" he finally inquired, in so peculiar a tone that Natty hardly recognized his voice.

"Adela Ross, sir," the child replied.

"You are the daughter of the lady and gen-

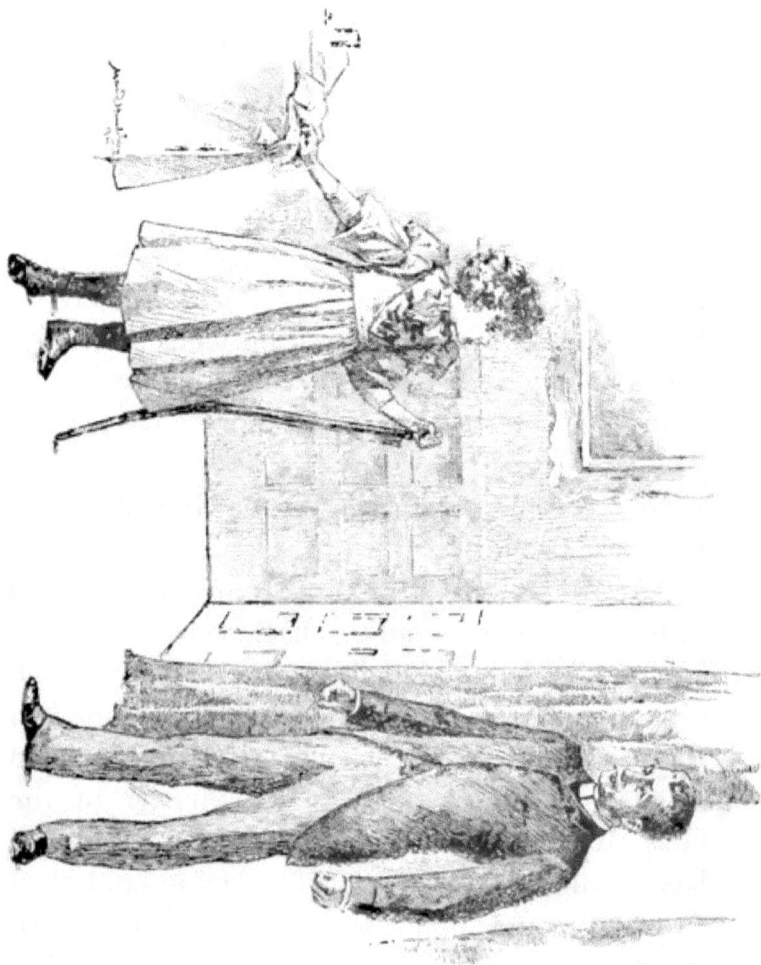

"SHE LAID DOWN HER KNIFE AND FORK, AND ROSE FROM HER SEAT"

tleman who have come to perform at Fenlowe
Hall?"

"Yes, sir; but mamma has not appeared yet.
She is not strong enough. Papa and I do everything."

The girl's lip quivered as she answered, and
her eyes were cast down, as if to hide a painful
emotion.

"Is she so ill that it grieves you to speak of
her?" asked Mr. Huntington.

"Oh no, sir; I hope she is not very ill. It is
not that. Please excuse me."

"Sit down, my dear. What is it that disturbs
you? I thought Natty was to make everything
pleasant during your call. Do you know what
the matter is, Natty?"

"Yes, sir, I do," said the boy, stoutly, although
Adela looked at him with beseeching eyes.

"Oh, Natty!" she murmured, ruefully.

"But I mustn't tell if she is not willing," the
boy added, promptly.

"I am sure there is nothing," said Mr. Huntington, "that she should be unwilling to let us
hear. Perhaps we can help her, Mrs. Barton
and I."

The house-keeper's kind heart was beating fast.
She had not seen her employer in so gracious a
mood for many a year.

14

"I think we may be told," the lawyer continued; and as Adela made no further attempt to remonstrate, Natty hastened to explain.

"She was saying, out in the river garden, that she felt as if it was wicked to have such a beautiful holiday all to herself, when her mother could not enjoy it too."

"Oh, Natty!" repeated Adela, dismayed and confused.

"There is no harm in that," said Mr. Huntington. "Do you understand what she means, Natty?"

"No, sir; not exactly. Yes, sir; I do—a little."

"Is your mother fond of gardens?" the lawyer inquired of Adela.

"I don't think she has been in many, sir—not many like yours. We go about a good deal, but mostly in large cities. We never were in such a pretty town as this before. And, oh, the lovely river, and the flowers!"

"And the pigsty," suggested Natty.

"Y—es," assented Adela, cautiously. "It is all so—interesting."

"Fortunately we can do something to relieve your anxiety," said Mr. Huntington. "Mrs. Barton, you will oblige me by inviting this little lady's mother and father to pass next Sunday with you. Natty, my lad, you shall invite the daughter. You can ramble around all day long, as you like, and take tea in the arbor on the river-bank if the air is mild enough. Tell your parents, my child, that they must pardon me if I do not join the party. I am not used to company, and you will amuse yourselves much better without me. And look here, Natty; before your friend goes to-day, you might gather a basket of flowers for her to carry to Mrs. Ross."

The unlooked-for turn of events made Mrs. Barton almost dizzy; and as for Natty, his eyes and mouth were widening to an alarming extent. Adela had no means of knowing how contrary to his ordinary conduct the lawyer's present behavior was, but she was deeply touched, and leaving the table, she ran to him and grasped one of his hands in both of her own. Tears were upon her cheeks as she cried:

"How good you are! Nobody else has been so good. Papa and mamma are sure, though Natty would not tell, that it was you who let us stay and perform in Fenlowe, and when they hear that they may come to the garden and enjoy themselves on Sunday, I don't know what they will say. I wish I could thank you properly, Mr. Huntington, but I can't. Papa will do that, and mamma, too, for me and for themselves."

The stern lawyer lifted the child in his arms, and held her close to him while he peered into her large brown eyes. Then, wonder of wonders, he bent his head and kissed her on the forehead, after which he set her down hurriedly, and abruptly left the room.

"Ah, my dear," said Mrs. Barton, "it is natural that he should be moved. I cannot tell you how much you look like some one he knew and cared for very much when he was younger."

"Do I, really, Mrs. Barton?"

"Indeed you do."

Adela would have asked more, but footsteps were heard, and Mr. Huntington came again before them.

"You take part in your father's performances," he said; "do you not, my child?"

"Oh yes, sir; I do a great many things."

"Tell your father that I shall give myself the pleasure of looking in to-morrow. I wish to see for myself what his exhibition is."

"He will be very glad. So will you, Mr. Huntington. It will make you laugh. I *think* it will make you laugh. It ought to. Everybody laughs—except that rude Mr. Mullins."

"I may not laugh, but I don't doubt I shall be pleased. And if your father desires to use me for the trick which disagreed with Mullins, he is welcome to do so."

"Oh no, sir; he would not think of that."

"Why not? It will show that a sensible man is not offended by it, whatever Mullins may say."

"You don't mean the rabbit, sir?"

"If the rabbit does not object, certainly."

"And the goose?"

"The goose, by all means."

"I will tell papa what you say," said Adela, dubiously; "but I don't believe he would ever do it—not to you. It wouldn't look at all natural," she added, with an air of grave reflection, "to see a goose come out of your neck."

"Tell him, and let him do as he chooses," were Mr. Huntington's last words as he again left them.

"He's sorry about something," said Adela, after he had gone. "He did not smile once, not even when we talked about the goose. But he will to-morrow afternoon. Nobody can help being merry when papa does his best, and he will do his very *best* best for Mr. Huntington. How happy we shall be!"

"I don't know whether I am awake or asleep!" exclaimed Mrs. Barton. "When he came and told us he was going to see the magic, I had to put my hand over my mouth to keep from screaming

out loud. My little girl, you can't realize what
you have done. You will not stay in Fenlowe
long, and when you go I suppose we shall never
see you again, but I believe your coming to-day
has brought a blessing on this sad house, and if
it lasts I will be thankful to you, my dear, all the
days of my life."

VI

ON Saturday afternoon Fenlowe Hall was
filled with the largest audience ever gathered
within its walls. The report that Mr. Huntington was to be present had flown about, and the
community were one and all on the alert to witness so remarkable an event as the reappearance
of their most distinguished townsman in a public place of amusement. Many who could not
gain admittance to the building stood about the
doorway, determined to behold at least the entrance of the recluse, if, indeed, the extraordinary rumor should be verified. On this point
there was still considerable doubt, and one individual did not hesitate to declare his opinion
that the story was an utter fabrication, unworthy of a moment's credence. This was Mr. Mullins, the surly lessee, who amused himself in the

vestibule by scoffing at the credulity of the populace.

"Lawyer Huntington patronize this miserable show!" he cried. "Not he. Do you think that after shutting himself up for ten whole years he would choose an occasion like this to come out of his shell? Get along with you! It's nothing but a trick of this juggling fellow to make folks curious and draw a big house."

The words had scarcely passed his lips when the tall form of Mr. Huntington was seen moving slowly down the street in the direction of the hall. Every tongue was hushed, and a silence fell on the multitude, although, but for the universal deference to the lawyer's feelings, and the knowledge that a noisy demonstration would be distasteful to him, the majority would have been disposed to cheer. He gravely acknowledged the salutations offered him from all sides, and carefully made his way through the throng which nearly blocked the porch. As he crossed the threshold, Mr. Mullins, greatly disconcerted, but preserving a good share of his natural audacity, drew up and addressed him thus:

"Glad to see you out and among us, sir; uncommon glad. But sorry you've been misled into coming to this stupid exhibition. There's nothing in it, I assure you, sir."

"Let me pass, if you please, Mr. Mullins," answered Mr. Huntington. "You are obstructing the passage."

Mullins stood aside, and watched the lawyer with a slight sense of uneasiness as he walked down the aisle and took the seat reserved for him. The gruff lessee did not exactly like it, and resolved to keep his eye on the unexpected visitor.

The entertainment began in due course, but it was a question for a time whether the performances on the stage or the stately figure in the centre of the audience claimed the greater degree of attention from those present. Little Adela's gentle charm soon asserted itself, however, and when she stepped into the body of the hall, followed by her father, and tripped lightly towards Mr. Huntington, the excitement rose to the highest possible pitch.

"Your own request, sir," said Mr. Ross, in an undertone, bending towards the lawyer; "but I will stop whenever you bid me."

"Go on," replied Mr. Huntington. "I am entirely at your service."

Whereupon the magician passed a hand over Mr. Huntington's head, and drew, or appeared to draw, from his neck a basket of assorted fruits, which Adela took and offered to the ladies who sat near.

"Here! here! that won't do!" was heard in
rough tones from the back of the hall, while
Mullins's burly shape was seen pushing forward.
"I won't allow it. What do you mean by playing your impudent pranks upon Lawyer Huntington?"

"Do not interfere, Mullins," ordered Mr. Huntington, sharply. "I am glad to testify that there
is nothing objectionable in this kind of amusement. Continue, Mr. Conjurer."

"But, sir—" urged Mullins.

"Be quiet, and make no further disturbance,"
said Mr. Huntington, so emphatically that the
mischief-maker was subdued for the moment,
and turned, discomfited, to resume his post of
observation at the rear. As he did so, the conjurer caught at his coat-pocket, and extracted
therefrom a little live pig, kicking its legs, twist-
ing its corkscrew of a tail, and squealing vigor-
ously as it was held high in the air. The spectators were wild with delight, while Mullins, in
a fury, rushed out of sight. Of all the witnesses,
Mr. Huntington was the only one that was not
convulsed with laughter.

The wizard fell to his work again, and began
taking out flowers and toys in profusion from
the favored visitor's sleeves and pockets, produc-
.ing finally a large bundle of cornucopiæ, or

"horns of plenty," overflowing with candies and tiny cakes.

"A fitting emblem, sir—generosity and bounty," said Mr. Ross, proceeding to distribute the confections.

Mr. Huntington beckoned to Adela, who was close at hand.

"I miss something," he said, so that only she could hear. "This is not what you promised me."

"Oh, sir," she answered, in the same low voice, "not the goose. I couldn't let papa do that. No, nor even the rabbit. But—"

She went nearer to him, and looked playfully in his face. Still he did not smile, but he returned her gaze in a manner that made those who watched him wonder at its earnestness. Suddenly Adela raised her hands and pulled apart the upper folds of his waistcoat.

"Why, Mr. Huntington, what can this be?" she exclaimed, drawing forth two white doves, which, as she threw them into the air, fluttered towards Mr. Ross, and presently perched upon his arm. This was the first display of sleight-of-hand that the child had attempted without aid, and the applause was unbounded.

"Tell your father," the lawyer whispered, when Adela was about returning to the stage, "to show us the pistol trick."

ADELA'S DOVE TRICK

She obeyed, and after calling two lads to assist him—one of whom, you may be sure, was Natty—the conjurer produced his weapon and the vase of goldfish. Their appearance was the signal for another outburst on the part of Mullins.

"This can't go on!" roared the obstreperous lessee. "I told you I wouldn't have the thing repeated. Stop it!"

"Ladies and gentlemen," said Mr. Ross, advancing to the edge of the platform, "you have heard the lessee's prohibition; but a person of higher authority in Fenlowe Hall than the lessee has called for this particular performance. I shall therefore not desist."

"I forbid it! I'll prosecute you!" shouted Mullins.

The necromancer cast a glance of inquiry at his supporter, who nodded affirmatively.

"But it is dangerous, Mr. Huntington," protested Mullins, as soon as he noticed the signal. "You will risk our lives if you let him keep on."

"That is sheer nonsense," said the lawyer, turning upon Mullins, "although I believe the same accusation has been freely made elsewhere, to Mr. Ross's injury. The pistol has always been a perfectly harmless toy, except once, when a reckless boy tampered with it. That was a piece of wilful and malicious mischief, and it

would be unlucky for the perpetrator if his misdeed were forced too strongly upon my attention. Finish your performance, Mr. Conjurer;
I think you will not be interrupted again."

It was now evident that Mr. Huntington had
taken the magician under his protection, and
though no one could guess at his motive, a prolonged clapping of hands gave assurance that
his intercession was warmly approved and in-
dorsed. Mullins fled from the room, followed
by jeers and cries of mockery. The entertainment proceeded agreeably; and when, just before the end, the lawyer rose to his feet and
asked to be heard in explanation of his presence
on this particular afternoon, every eye was bent
on him, and the silence was profound as he uttered these words:

"My friends and fellow-townsfolk, I have
departed from my customary course of life, and
come hither to-day to overrule and if possible to
repair an act of injustice. The gentleman to
whom we are indebted for our present diversion
came to Fenlowe with the intention of remaining
several weeks. He had strong reasons, with which
I heartily sympathize, for desiring to give in this
hall a series of exhibitions; but the lessee, choos-
ing to be affronted at a trifling pleasantry, took
it upon himself to deny the stranger that privi-

lege, and to deprive you all of several excellent
entertainments. These facts came to my knowledge through a youthful member of our community, who could not bear to see such a wrong
done without striving hard to avert it. I am
obliged to him for reminding me of my duty in
this instance, and I shall take care hereafter that
personal spite shall not be a reason for refusing
the accommodations of Fenlowe Hall to any ap-
plicant. I have endeavored to make it apparent
that I approve Mr. Ross's performances, and that
the charge spread about to his discredit—of care-
lessness in using weapons — is without foundation. Unless Mr. Mullins is prepared to give up
the lease of this building, he will reverse his decision and place no obstacles in this gentleman's
course. I wish our visitor every success, and
you, ladies and gentlemen, a cordial good-afternoon."

Having spoken thus, Mr. Huntington went rapidly out, while the listeners unitedly signified
their satisfaction with his remarks, and their determination to uphold the object of them. Mr.
Ross was deeply grateful, and his voice was unsteady when he next attempted to use it. He
said, frankly, that he was not accustomed to such
kindness, and felt unable to express his obligation becomingly; but he hoped to find some

effective means of proving before he left Fenlowe that he was not wholly unworthy of the
interest and good-will bestowed upon him and
his family.

The opportunity was nearer than he thought.

VII

"She is a dear little creature," said Mrs. Barton, while conversing alone with Mr. Huntington on the following morning. "I wish some
good person would adopt her and take her out
of those unsettled, rambling ways."

"I understand you," the lawyer replied; "but
I should be unequal to so hard a trial. Her face
would be a constant reproach to me."

"Don't say that, sir. I am sure you did everything that man could do to find Miss Helen
—Mrs. Greaves, I mean."

"When it was too late," said Mr. Huntington,
mournfully. "No; the child is closely attached
to her parents, and they would probably refuse
to part with her for any consideration. They
could not be expected to submit to such a sacrifice. But I hope to see her many times while
she remains here. Make her visit as pleasant as

you can, Mrs. Barton, so that she will wish to come again."

He had quite forgotten his statement to Adela, two days before, that he could not personally receive any of the guests on Sunday; but Mrs. Barton remembered it, and drew hopeful conclusions from his change of mind.

Mr. and Mrs. Ross, with Adela, were ushered by Natty, about eleven o'clock, into the stately Huntington mansion. Their entrance produced an effect upon those of the neighbors who witnessed it not less remarkable than that created by the lawyer's appearance in Fenlowe Hall. For more than ten years he had admitted no visitors to his residence, except for necessary business purposes, and nobody comprehended why the first relaxation of the rule should be for the benefit of an unknown family whose vocation assuredly could not serve as a powerful recommendation to favor. But Mrs. Barton was in no uncertainty upon the subject. She did her best to make the strangers contented and comfortable, and her success was such that Mrs. Ross's usually pale face glowed with animation, while every trace of uneasiness vanished from her husband's features. Adela, for her part, danced about and sang so cheerfully as to cause all the party to forget that there was such a thing as care in the world.

Early in the afternoon, as they were sitting in the arbor on the bank of the river, they saw Mr. Huntington approaching through the orchard. Adela ran to meet him.

"I knew you would come," she cried, taking his hand to lead him to the others. "Natty was afraid you could not, but I told him you were too good to stay away when mamma wanted so much to thank you. Mamma would have been distressed if she had not seen you."

"And you, my child?" asked Mr. Huntington.

"Oh, I am a little girl, and can go anywhere and do anything. I should have tried to find you. I hope you would not have been angry; would you?"

"No, my dear; but that is because you are good, not I."

"Ah no; I am not too little to know who is good. Anybody that is kind to mamma is good, and you have been the kindest of all. It made me—you mustn't say anything about it, but it made me cry, yesterday, when papa told her what you had done to help us to stay here, and get her well."

"Why, how can a person be good who makes you cry?"

"It doesn't hurt to cry like that," she explained, laughing joyously. "Now here are my papa and mamma, ever so glad to see you."

In a few simple and sincere words the invalid conveyed her acknowledgment of the important service which the lawyer had rendered. Mr. Huntington was struck by the refinement and delicacy of her manner. He knew very little about the class to which wizards and conjurers belong, but his first thought was that if Adela's destiny bound her to a career of publicity, it was fortunate that she was under the guidance of so well-bred a gentlewoman.

"To tell you the truth, sir," said Mr. Ross, whose manner was less reserved than his wife's, "we haven't been able to account for the consideration you have shown us. It is not a common experience with us, and, indeed, people in our line of occupation do not look for it; but it is none the less gratifying for that, you can well believe."

"If you are indebted to anybody," said Mr. Huntington, seating himself in the arbor, "it is to Master Natty, in the first place. He told me about Mullins's freak of ill-humor, and as I am the owner of the hall, it seemed proper that I should interfere. Yet I am not sure that I should have gone to the entertainment if I had not seen your daughter while she was here as

15

Natty's guest. It needs a strong persuasion to entice an old hermit out of his solitude, but I could not resist her."

"She has been a blessing to us," exclaimed Mr. Ross, "ever since we—"

"All her life," interposed Mrs. Ross, breaking in upon her husband's sentence.

"I do not doubt it," said Mr. Huntington. "I have known one who was not unlike her, and who at her age was the joy and brightness of all around her."

"I beg your pardon, sir," said Mr. Ross; "may I ask if she was your child?"

"My child? No; it was my sister Helen."

"Helen!" exclaimed Mr. and Mrs. Ross together, with a look of surprise.

"That was her name," said the lawyer, quietly.

"Would you kindly tell me her full name?" inquired Mr. Ross. "Believe me, I do not ask in idle curiosity."

"Helen Huntington," was the reply. "Or, if you mean her name after marriage, it was Helen Greaves."

Mrs. Ross drew a quick breath, and folding her arms tightly about Adela, pressed the child to her breast. Mr. Ross, after a moment's pause, spoke hurriedly to his wife, with an effort at composure which was far from successful.

"Do not hold her, my love," he said; "she must leave us for a little while." Turning to Adela, he added: "Go with Natty, dear; he will entertain you somewhere else. I have something to tell Mr. Huntington which you need not hear —not yet—not yet."

Adela's eyes grew big and round with wonder, but she kissed Mrs. Ross, and obeyed in silence, taking Natty's hand, and seeming to direct rather than follow him.

"It is a very serious matter," continued the magician. "I have no right—and no desire—to make suggestions in this place, but perhaps we ought to speak with Mr. Huntington entirely alone."

"Mrs. Barton has been in my family twenty years," said the lawyer, greatly astonished. "I can think of nothing that should be withheld from her."

"Then, sir, though it is a hard thing for me to say, my duty requires me to tell you that Adela is not our daughter—"

"Not yours?" exclaimed Mr. Huntington.

"And that her true name is Helen Greaves."

"Are you trifling with me?" cried the lawyer, springing to his feet.

"Heaven forbid, sir! I would give everything I own in the world to keep the secret forever, if

I could do so justly; but I am bound in honor to let you hear the truth. Ten years ago, when we were travelling in South Carolina, we passed through a small town called Greensborough. We stopped at a hotel in which a Northern lady had just died. We never saw her, but the landlord's wife, one of the best and tenderest of women, told us she had been brought there for her health, and then deserted by her husband—a brilliant but worthless adventurer named Greaves. She left a little girl, who was then only a few months old. The landlady was full of compassion, but she was not prosperous, and after we had been there some days she yielded to our proposal that we should adopt the child. We did so, and— I need not say any more, sir. You can tell better than I who she really is, but it will almost break our hearts if we must lose her."

Mr. Huntington had dropped into his seat again, and he now leaned forward, resting his elbows on a table, and his face fell upon his hands.

"Answer me honorably," he said, in a broken voice. "You don't know what this means to me. Have you any papers or other articles connected with the birth of the child?"

"Several letters, sir, a few pieces of clothing, and some trinkets. We always keep them by us."

"Why have you made no effort to discover her relations?"

"We have made all in our power, but the indications were very imperfect. The letters were dated from Washington, and were not fully signed. They were evidently from the lady's brother. The only name at the end was Robert."

"It is mine; but why did you change that of the child?"

"We were led to believe it was the mother's wish. She had been in terror lest her husband should get possession of the infant, and use it as a means—"

"I understand; as a means of extorting money."

"Precisely, sir. The landlady, who had been in the poor sufferer's confidence, begged us to conceal everything until we could trace the child's family. So we called her Adela Ross— Adela being my wife's name, also—and for a long time we spared no effort to find the brother who wrote the letters in our possession. Our means were limited, and we failed. The search was discontinued years ago. But I may say, without fear of contradiction, that the little one has been tenderly reared, and you can learn from her own lips if she has ever been unhappy."

"God bless you! I am sure she has not. You will let me examine the relics of which you speak? I wish the identification to be complete, and then—"

"Oh, Mr. Huntington," interrupted Mrs. Barton, "what more can you want than a single look at the dear child's face? She is your sister Helen alive again."

"Indeed it seems so, Mrs. Barton; and now I have the explanation of the singular influence her gentle voice and sweet smile have had upon me. It was a happy day when your son brought her to my lonely house."

"For you, sir, but not for us," said Mr. Ross, dejectedly.

Before an answer could be given, Adela's voice was heard at a short distance.

"May I come now, papa? Natty has caught me a funny turtle, that shuts up its head and tail, and makes a box of itself. I'll give it to you, papa, and if Mr. Mullins is disagreeable again, you can take it out of his mouth some evening."

She ran into the arbor, full of gay vivacity; but the mirth faded from her face when she saw that Mrs. Ross was weeping. Dropping her new prize, she sprang to her protectress, crying:

"Mamma, mamma, what is the matter? What has happened?"

"Something strange has happened," said the sorrowing lady, endeavoring to control herself. "Something fortunate for you, Adela, but very sad for me. We have just learned that Mr. Huntington is your uncle."

"My uncle!" exclaimed the child, in amazement, and looking curiously at the lawyer. "Are you my uncle? Are you—are you my mamma's brother?"

"I am, my dear," he answered; "I am your mother's brother, but not this lady's. She—"

"What do you mean?" demanded Adela. "I cannot understand."

"Come hither, my love," he replied, drawing her to him. "I am truly your uncle, and I thank God that I have found you. You are the only one of my near kindred left. My home is yours, and you must never leave me."

"Mamma, what is he saying?" she cried, breaking from him, and rushing again to Mrs. Ross. "I am your little girl, and papa's, and nobody else's."

"My darling, we must think of what is right and just. Mr. Huntington will love you dearly, and will never separate us wholly, I believe. To-night I will tell you all that we have just learned. You will let her stay with us, sir, while we are in Fenlowe?"

"I will always stay with you," declared the child, in a passion of grief and fear. "Do not send me away, mamma. Oh, dear mamma, I shall die if you do!"

For a moment nothing more was heard than her piteous sobs, as she lay in Mrs. Ross's arms. Then the lawyer spoke again, in faltering accents.

"It would be hard indeed if the heart of my sister's child were turned against me on the very day of her restoration. Listen to me, dear. This must be your home, as I have said; but I have no wish to take you from her who has cherished and guarded you all your life. Your strong affection for her shows how worthily she has tried to fill the place of the mother whom you never knew. It is too early to speak decisively, but I am confident we can arrange a plan by which Mrs. Ross will consent to watch over you hereafter, as she has always done."

"You will not keep mamma away from me? She *is* my mamma, you know," said the trembling girl, still anxious and alarmed.

"Not for the world, if she will remain with us. Are you, Mr. Ross, much attached to your present calling?"

"Frankly, sir," answered the magician, "it was pleasant, when we were younger, to wander

"'I WILL ALWAYS STAY WITH YOU,' DECLARED THE CHILD"

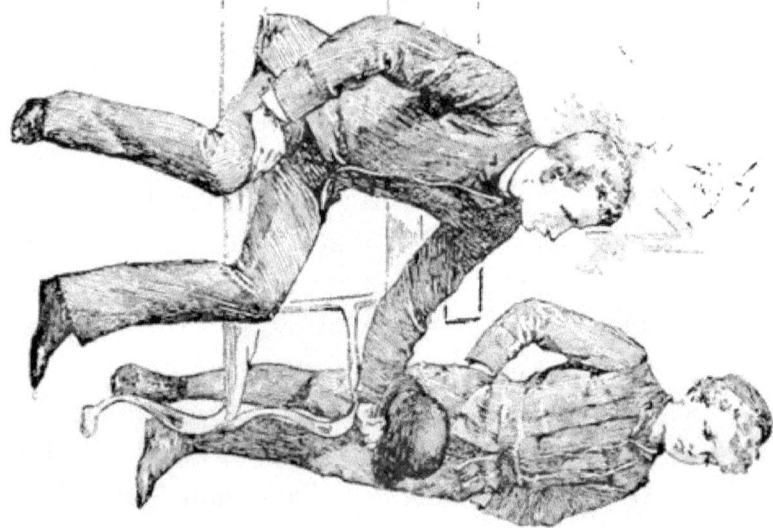

about the country, earning our humble livelihood by providing amusement for others; but the charm does not last forever, and the chances of success are uncertain, as you have seen. Yet, at my age, it is not easy to strike into a new path."

"Leave that to me," said Mr. Huntington. "My interests are large, and I shall have no difficulty, I think, in offering you a satisfactory occupation. Nothing that I can do will ever repay what I owe you."

"Oh, Mr. Huntington," exclaimed the still bewildered child, "do you mean that mamma shall rest here, and get well and strong?"

"I hope so."

"And papa shall have no more trouble?"

"Not if you and I can prevent it."

"Then you are the best gentleman I ever knew, and I am willing to be your little girl, too. But it is so wonderful. More wonderful than anything I have seen you do, papa."

"Yes, dear," Mr. Ross acknowledged; "and it is all real, too, though I can hardly believe it yet. We are not the enchanters in this case. Natty Barton is the magician who has brought it all about."

So every one felt and said. Natty's honest face glowed as he listened to the praise and thanks lavished upon him, and his mother was proud of the happy consequences of her boy's kindly actions. As Mr. Huntington had assured them, there was no difficulty in finding a suitable field for Mr. Ross's activity, and his industry and fidelity made him a valuable agent in conducting portions of his wealthy patron's private business. He took charge of considerable property in Fenlowe, including the hall from which so unfair an attempt had been made to banish him; for the owner decided, after investigation, that it was not wise to lease that establishment again to a man of Mr. Mullins's unpleasant humors. Many persons were forward in expressing doubts as to the propriety of prolonging the connection between Robert Huntington's niece and her former guardians, whose recent calling could not be forgotten, and whose social grade was supposed to be far below that to which the newly discovered heiress had risen. But the lawyer sturdily rejected these suggestions, declaring that the conduct of the kind-hearted conjurer and his wife in fostering the orphan child had been generous and noble; and that, as they had brought back the sunshine to his home, he would do his best to keep the clouds away from their future life. He never had cause to repent his resolution. Mrs. Ross's devotion was constant, and the young girl's destiny was secure in her tender and loving care. Adela Ross gave place in name to Helen Huntington (since her uncle could not bear to hear her called Helen Greaves), but her sweet and gracious spirit remained unchanged, and was the light and cheer of the household in which she was treasured. The years passed by, filled with tranquil happiness to those who were brought together by the events here narrated, and with a never-fading recollection of the beneficent results of Natty Barton's magic.

OUR UGLY IDOL

I

BITTERS

UGLY? Well, since you ask me, I will admit he's not a handsome dog, but we never think about that, one way or the other. As to his being a proper dog for the parlor, I can only say that if there was a better room than the parlor anywhere in our house, he would always be welcome to it. Would you like to know why? Then you shall hear it all from the beginning.

I was just fourteen years old when I became the owner of Scar. He had a history before he was given to me, which I must tell first, in order to introduce him properly. Good dogs have as much right to an introduction as good boys and girls, or grown-up people, for that matter. If you should see Scar go through the ceremony of a polite introduction, you would say—but never mind ; it is too early to speak of such things as his manners in company.

When I mention good dogs I do not mean that Scar always belonged to that class. Most of us thought at one time that he was a very bad dog. His first master lived at the corner of our street, and kept a shop with a large window, on which the words " Fruit Store " were painted. When I was about ten years old I went in there once and inquired if I could buy a watermelon. Laura, my little sister, was with me. The place was full of rough men, who looked as if they had no interest in watermelons or any kind of fruit. They all began to laugh, but the shopkeeper was very civil and good-natured. He said he had sold his watermelons, but he had a nice lemon to offer me, if that would do. I supposed it would have to do, because I saw nothing else that looked like fruit. I did not much want it, but the man seemed so sorry about the melon that I hated to go without taking something. When I asked what the price was he said he couldn't think of charging anything, as that was my first visit. So I thanked him, and Laura thanked him too very prettily, upon which he gave her a lump of sugar and some little sticks of cinnamon which he took from a saucer, and wrapped up in a piece of pa-

per.   Then he asked if we would like to see his
beautiful dog.

Of course I said we should like it, and he told
a boy to bring Bitters, which I thought was a
strange name for a dog, and particularly for a
beautiful dog.   But when Bitters appeared I was
still more astonished.   He was a bull-terrier, all
tan - color, with dreadfully impatient eyes and
quarrelsome teeth.   He was covered with dirt,
and had the most disagreeable appearance of any
dog I ever met.

"Isn't he a picture?" said the shopman.

I supposed he loved his dog, as everybody does,
and I didn't wish to hurt his feelings ; so I answered: "I don't know much about that kind of
dog.   Perhaps he isn't very well to-day."

"Oh, he's in prime condition," said the man.
"He killed sixteen rats this morning, and whipped a dog twice his size only an hour ago."

"Dear me," said I ; "he *does* look a little fierce."

"Bless you, no," answered the man.   "He had
lots of fierceness in him when he was a puppy,
but we drove it all into his ears and tail, and
then we cut them off.   Now he's as gentle as an
angel baby."

When Laura heard this she stepped forward to
caress him; but he suddenly curled up his lip
like a cockle - shell, and snarled in such an ill-

tempered way that I thought it best to jump in front of his mouth. It was well I did so, for he made a quick snap, and tore away a strip of my trousers. It might have been a strip of me, which would have been bad; but if it had been a strip of Laura, that would have been horrible.

The shopman gave Bitters a frightful kick, and scolded the boy savagely for not minding the rope with which the dog was held. Then he turned to me very anxiously, and I noticed that his voice was unsteady as he spoke.

"I wouldn't have had it happen for a hundred dollars," he said. "But he didn't hurt you? No, nor frighten you either, I'll be bound. You are a brave little man, to stand between danger and your sister. If ever I part with Bitters, you shall have him—there! But now, young gentleman, you'd better go. Much obliged for your visit, but this isn't quite the place for you. Don't think hard of Bitters. Bitters is a good dog."

But this is not what I meant by a proper introduction to Scar. It may stand as *my* introduction to him, if you please, for, as you have guessed, Bitters and Scar are one and the same person. If you have studied French, you will permit me to refer to him as Scar, *né* Bitters. But I wish him to have a different sort of introduction to *you*, lest you should be too severely

prejudiced against him at the outset. I must
acknowledge that after that first interview I
made no attempt to keep up the acquaintance,
and in fact we did not come together again till
close upon the end of my thirteenth year, when
a startling event occurred.

Papa had often spoken about the misfortune
of having a common bar-room (for that is what
the "fruit store" truly was) so near our house,
but said it was one of the troubles that could not
always be avoided in a large city. One night
there was a great disturbance at the corner. I
slept too soundly to hear the pistol-shots and the
breaking glass; but next morning we were told
there had been a terrible fight, and that the
keeper of the place had been nearly killed. He
did, in fact, die a few days later. The most
remarkable thing was that the murderer was
caught and brought to justice by—whom do you
think? By nobody but Bitters, the bull-terrier.
During the fight he fastened himself upon the
man who had struck down his master, and never
let go his grip until the police came. The poor
dog was cruelly cut and mangled, but nothing
could loosen his hold; and although he was half
insensible, they had to pry his mouth open with
one of those patent corkscrews that look like the
letter X, before they could get him away.

Bitters and his master were taken to the same
hospital, for the liquor-dealer was well off, and
could pay for his fancies. The doctors did all
they could for them both, but the man's health
had been ruined by evil habits, and he died. Bitters had not been well brought up, it is true; but
at least he was not a drinking dog, and his constitution was sound. So he eventually got well.

We first heard of the barkeeper's death and
burial in this way: A woman called one evening
and asked if she could speak with Mr. Etheridge
and his eldest son. Papa went alone to see who
it was and what she wanted, but presently he
sent for mamma and me.

"This is the widow of Mr. Kerrigan, who lived
at the corner," said my father. "She has a proposal to make to Arthur."

"Indeed yes, sir and ma'am," said the woman,
who spoke with a brogue which I don't think I
will try to imitate. "That is the young gentleman, and this it is I have to tell. When my poor
Michael was settling his affairs, just before he
died, he says to me, 'Matilda Kerrigan, there's
Bitters. It is hard upon me to give up the dog,
but it's a matter of three years ago that I promised if I ever parted with him he should be made
over to young Mister Etheridge, for I believe
that lad has the spirit in him to manage the

16

beast, and the heart to train him up as becomes
a dog of his merit. Do you mind,' says Michael,
'the day he stood up against Bitters, man to
man, and never budged while the brute was making mince-meat of his pantaloons?' Often would
my husband talk about it, sir and ma'am, almost
as proud of your son, asking your pardon for the
liberty, as he was of the bull-terrier; and *him* he
looked upon as if the dog was own twins with
our little Michael, they being the same age to a
week."

I saw my father lift his eyebrows, and mamma
look rather uncomfortable — I presume at the
idea of my having anything to do with so fero-
cious an animal. It was not an agreeable idea to
me either, though I naturally felt interested in
Mrs. Kerrigan's story.

" When Michael was buried," she went on,
" the dog was able to limp about, and nothing
we could do would keep him from going to the
funeral. Hard words he laughed at, and when
the undertaker showed him a whip he lifted his
lip till you saw the black mischief creeping all
around his mouth. So he was allowed to make a
separate procession by himself, under the hearse,
interfering with nobody so long as nobody inter-
fered with him. But it was great trouble he
gave us at the grave, trying to leap in, the faith-

"'THAT IS THE YOUNG GENTLEMAN, AND THIS IT IS I HAVE TO TELL.'"

ful dumb creature, and begging to be covered
out of sight with his master. Then my heart
went straight to him, and I paid half a dollar
each to Jane Rooney's two boys to bring him
home, and a losing job it was for them, the doctor and the ointment for Jimmy Rooney's legs
costing more than the whole bargain money.
And now, sir and ma'am, it's filled with shame I
am at what comes next. Well did I remember
Michael's command, but the pride that was in
me at owning the noblest beast in the ward held
my hand, and I took no heed of my honest duty.
'A comfort to my loneliness he shall be,' says I,
'with visitors coming from all parts to admire
the marks of his wounds in the fight.'"

"You are quite right, Mrs. Kerrigan," said my
father. "Don't give him up on any account.
No one else could appreciate him so well as
you do."

"Thank you, sir, for the kind words," replied
Mrs. Kerrigan. "But I've had a warning. Not
one warning only, but many. The first night
after the burying I tied him in the yard, as usual,
and in the morning he was gone, leaving nothing
but the end of his rope. We hunted till the
afternoon, when a gateman came from the cemetery, very angry, telling me to take the dog from
Mr. Kerrigan's lot, or they would shoot him. We

got him home again, and fastened him with a
chain, but the power that's in him you'd not believe. He broke it short off; and when we sent
the next day, knowing by this time where to
hunt for him, we found him stretched on the
sods, looking weary and downcast, but not dis-
contented till he was pulled away. Then we
locked him in the kitchen, and again no use, for
at daylight it was empty, except a few hairs
sticking to the broken glass in the window. And
so it went on. Sometimes we managed to keep
him overnight, but sooner or later he was off,
and nothing could stay him. Once he jumped
from the second story to the street, and once
he crawled up from the cellar to the sidewalk
through the tunnel while we were taking in coals.
How he ever found his way is the wonder of
wonders, for it is full four miles to the grave-
yard, and Bitters, being a bull-terrier, has no
nose to help him, sir, as you know quite well,
ma'am. But Bitters is no common dog; indeed,
indeed he is not."

Perhaps it was because I had lately been reading of a dog in Edinburgh, Scotland, who showed
the same devotion to his dead master; but whatever was the reason, something suddenly made
me feel very differently towards Bitters from
what I had ever felt before. I wanted to say so

at once, but papa checked me, and Mrs. Kerrigan brought her story to a close.

"Now I see my way clear, and it makes me tremble to think of the harm that might have come from my disobeying Michael's last words. And I made up my mind to-day to do what is right and dutiful. The dog is young Mister Etheridge's from this hour. A fine creature he is, and a delight he'll be to his new owner. It does distress me to let him go, with his playfulness and his pretty ways, but I know he will be well treated and respected in this house. Nobody could help taking kindly to Bitters. You say the word, sir, and I'll leave him here this very night."

My father is a most considerate man, and I knew he did not like to let Mrs. Kerrigan see the difference between our opinion of Bitters and her own. Moreover, as he told me afterwards, he was unwilling to make light of her superstitious notions about the warning, or to alarm her by sending her away with a positive refusal. He said to her:

"Madam, it would be impossible to receive such a guest as your bull-terrier without making some preparation, and indeed your generous offer deserves more reflection than I can give it at this moment. I will call on you to-morrow evening, and will then let you know our decision in the matter."

Then, observing an expression of disappointment on her face, he added, "I assure you we are greatly struck by your dog's courage and endurance, and especially his rare fidelity."

Our visitor looked as if she wondered how anybody could hesitate when such a splendid chance was freely presented, but she simply answered thus: "No doubt, sir and ma'am, you feel the responsibility of taking charge of a dog like Bitters, and of course it *does* fall heavy upon a young person. But my husband was clearheaded, and when it came to sporting animals his judgment was sound. He wouldn't have picked out your son without good reason. Besides, there's the warnings."

As soon as she had gone, my mother said: "There is nothing to be done but to make the refusal as easy as possible, and not allow the poor woman to know what an awful monster that dog is in our sight. She evidently thinks it one of the greatest treasures on the earth."

My father looked steadily at me, and reflected for a moment before he answered.

"This is my idea," he said at last: "we will have a family parliament on the subject to-morrow afternoon; your uncle Richard shall come to dinner, Arthur, and take part in the debate. I promise to listen carefully to all that may be said on both sides of the question, and my judgment shall be impartial. Don't you think that will be better than to settle it hastily now?"

"Oh yes, indeed, papa," I cried; "much better, if mamma is willing."

"Quite willing," said mamma, smiling; "but you must not expect me to speak in favor of accepting Bitters."

Then I went to bed, eagerly looking forward to the next day's family parliament, at which I meant to plead with all my might for the poor animal, which seemed so much in need of my protection. And if I must fail, I thought to myself, it should not be for want of hard trying.

II

SCAR

By the time our meeting was held on the following afternoon I had forgotten almost everything there was unpleasant about the dog in my admiration of his virtues of bravery and fidelity. Uncle Richard came promptly, and told us he had already constituted himself a committee to make inquiries in the neighborhood, but he would not tell us whether he had formed any opinion or not. At four o'clock papa invited mamma, Uncle Richard, and me into his study, and asked us to take places at his large table.

"I have called this assemblage together," he said, "because it seems proper to give Arthur a fair hearing. Last night he was rather too confused and excited to express himself clearly. Now let us listen to what he has to say."

I had a great deal to say—more, I am afraid, than mamma was pleased to hear. But she was very patient, and listened kindly while I told about the dog in Scotland that had become famous for acting almost exactly as Bitters had done, and asked if it was not possible that a creature so fearless and so true to its master might have other good qualities which we could find out by looking for them diligently. Then I pointed to our picture of the Education of an Eastern Prince, where there is a lion, very majestic, but very gentle, without any fastening, and surrounded by children. I said I thought if a lion could be made so mild by careful training, a bull-terrier could surely be tamed.

"I see, my dear," said mamma, good-naturedly: "you want to be the Eastern Prince."

"No, mamma," I said. "Baby Daisy shall be an Eastern Princess, if you please; I will be only the keeper."

"But a lion is a noble-looking beast," said mamma, "and this is such a hideous thing!"

So he was; I could not deny that; but after considering a little, I said: "He wouldn't be *quite* so ugly as he is if his head had not been cut while he was defending his master. I remember, mamma, what you have always told us about honorable scars."

Mamma laughed, and gave an odd look at Uncle Richard, who had been wounded badly in the face during the war.

"Oho, young gentleman!" exclaimed my uncle, "so you mean to bring me in as an example and an argument."

"No, Uncle Richard," I answered, feeling not at all comfortable. "I couldn't do that; at least, I did not mean to, only just at the moment—"

"I see," he said, making it easy by interrupting me. "It was natural enough. But, Arthur, your mother does not object so much to the dog's appearance as to his violent temper and cross disposition."

"I know it," said I, "but all that might be changed. Uncle Richard, I thought you would be on my side. Oh, mamma, I *should* like to try; I should be so proud if I could reform him."

It turned out that Uncle Richard *was* on my side, and papa not much against me; and the end of it was that mamma put away her unwilling-ness, and I was allowed to take Bitters, with the understanding that if I could not do anything with him in a month I should give up the at-tempt. I confess that when he was brought into our yard at the end of a strong, heavy chain, my resolution was shaken. He was indeed an awful object. His lower jaw seemed as if it must have been intended for a dog several sizes bigger, and his fore-legs were curved like a pair of parenthesis marks, or a barrel-hoop cut in two. His face had always been painful to look at, but now it was ten times worse, owing to the blows and slashes he had received. Then there was one long seam stretching from the side of his head down to where his tail ought to commence. Uncle Richard, who was formerly a brigadier-general, said there was more scar than dog, but it was no disgrace, as he had been cut to pieces in loyal combat. That first gave me the idea of calling him Scar. None of us could bear the name of Bitters, and Scar suited him exactly. Everybody would be sure to ask what it meant, and I could have the opportunity of telling his story, and letting people know there was more good in him than you would suspect from his outward looks.

Scar was so fierce and unfriendly, and so eager all the time to break loose, that for several days I could do nothing with him. I have no doubt he was always thinking how he could get back to the burial-ground. He sneered at every word of kindness I spoke to him, and if I scolded, he put on a look of scorn such as very few animals except a full-blooded bull-terrier can show. I read a great many books on dogs, but found nothing in them that made any impression on him, and I learned my first practical lesson at the expense of a terrible fright.

Freddy and Laura, my young brother and sister, had been warned never to go near the spot where Scar was fastened, but our baby, Daisy, was such a little thing that nobody dreamed of her getting into danger. Imagine what I felt when I came in one day after school, by the back gate, and saw Daisy lying on the ground entirely mixed up with the dog, her arms around his neck, and one of his paws all tangled in her curly hair. My heart went to my mouth, I can tell you. I hardly dared to stir, but as I stood staring at them, Daisy began to laugh, and I could see the bristles wiggle at the end of Scar's back, where the tail would have joined the body if it hadn't been cut short off. That was as near as he could come to a wag, and I believe he meant to tell me there was nothing to be alarmed about, and that Daisy was safe in his society. When I went straight to him, without stopping to think how cross he generally was, and pulled him away from her, he did not make the least objection, and only blinked his queer little eyes, as much as to say, " Oh, if you are going to take that tone with me, and act as a master ought to act, and not be afraid of me, I suppose I must submit." And that was exactly what I did.

From that moment I had no trouble with Scar. He was as yielding as if he had never known what obstinacy was. He always understood that he belonged to me and nobody else, but he seemed to have the greatest fondness for Daisy. She could take all sorts of liberties with him, and the more she took the better pleased he was. I believe it was because she was the first one to go to him without any fear, and make a playfellow of him.

Pretty soon I began to teach him tricks. Some people say bull-terriers are dull and stupid, and that their foreheads are so low they have no room for brains. That wasn't so with Scar. He had plenty of brains somewhere. Maybe they

"MY HEART WENT TO MY MOUTH—I HARDLY DARED TO STIR"

were down in his lower jaw, where there was room enough for anything. He was willing to learn all that I could teach him, and he grew quite vain as his education progressed. In less than six months he was the talk of our neighborhood. Mrs. Kerrigan came once to see him, but she did not like him at all in his new character. She said I had made a French poodle of him, and that he was fit only for a circus, and would never be worth anything in a fight. But I didn't want him to fight any more, now that he was my dog.

We took off his chain after the first few weeks, and he made no attempt to run away. But one afternoon, when we were out driving, and Scar was following the carriage, we happened to pass the gate of a large cemetery. In an instant he left us, and disappeared in one of the avenues. It was easy to understand where he had gone. With mother's permission, I inquired where Mr. Kerrigan was buried, and we all went in the direction that was pointed out. As we drew near a particular enclosure we saw Scar before he saw us; and what do you think he was doing? He was going through his best tricks, one after another, all alone on his old master's grave. I wondered with all my heart what could be passing in the poor dog's mind. I asked mamma if it was possible that he thought he could convey

some idea of his accomplishments—of which he
was so proud—to his former owner, lying there
beneath the earth. Mamma said it might be so,
but on one could tell with certainty. She spoke
more kindly to Scar than I had ever before heard
her. He stopped performing at once, and looked
at us in a puzzled, inquiring way. I called him,
and after reflecting an instant he followed us
slowly, stopping every little while, however, as
if he wished he could persuade us to remain there
with him ; but he did not lose sight of us. Once
outside the cemetery, he realized what his true
duty was, and trotted after the carriage as steadily
as ever. Since then we have seen nothing in
Scar to make us think of what he was in the
days when he was young and kept bad company.

"Nothing except his ugliness," did you say ?
Well, as I told you before, no one in this family
cares much about that, or ever considers whether
he is ugly or not. We love him too well to want
him changed in any particular. There is something you haven't heard yet.

The next summer after he came to us I had
that bad attack of typhus-fever, as you may remember, and to help me over it father took us
all yachting up and down Long Island Sound.
One day, when we were stopping near New
London, I was lying on deck in a long chair,

with Scar at my feet, and the other children playing all around. Father and mother and Uncle
Richard were in the cabin, out of the sun. Every
one of the crew had gone ashore except a single
man to keep watch. I was not well enough to
notice much of what was going on, so I understood very little of how it happened; but I knew
there was a great cry and a splash, and then,
turning myself about, I saw Daisy struggling in
the water. I was too weak to lift myself, and
neither Freddy nor Laura could do anything, of
course. I called to the watchman as loud as I
could, "Jump! jump!" But he looked at me,
as pale as marble, and cried, "I can't, Master
Arthur; I can't swim a stroke." Only think of
it, and he a good sailor, too! But he was over
the side and in a boat with wonderful speed.

Quick as he was, however, there was somebody
quicker. Like an echo to Daisy's splash, I heard
another, and there was Scar banging the surface
of Long Island Sound with his crooked paws, and
holding Daisy's dress in his great mouth. I could
hardly believe my eyes, for Scar hated water
like medicine, and would not even be washed
without making a mighty fuss; and there's many
a bull-terrier would sooner drown than swim a
stroke for his life. But there he was—I don't
know how to tell it—coughing, sneezing, splutter-

ing, kicking out all ways at once, but never letting go his hold of Daisy's frock. Everything seemed to take place together, at the same moment. Father and mother and Uncle Richard came running from below just as the sailor picked up Daisy and dragged her into the boat. In a minute more she was in mamma's arms, and we were all happy, though everybody was crying.

Suddenly I thought of Scar. He was not with us; but I heard a strange spattering noise, and looking hastily around, I saw the dear dog fighting blindly against the waves many yards away from the yacht. He was plunging around in a little circle, making no headway at all, while his big underjaw scooped in mouthfuls of salt-water, which I knew were choking him. For an instant his little eyes looked straight into mine. He made a sort of bound, and then fell back. Oh, poor dear Scar! I was very weak, too weak to keep my senses, and—and I'm foolish about it yet, I suppose, but I can't tell you any more for a minute or two. Please wait a little, and you shall hear the end.

You must not think any the worse of me for fainting. I know very well that boys have no business to faint when they are nearly grown-up men, and especially when they own a dog like

Scar, who sets them an example of pluck and grit. But remember how ill I had been. And then to see Daisy in such danger, and my faithful dog lifting himself up out of the waves to say good-bye to me, and everybody screaming—except Scar, for he would die a hundred times over before crying out once—it was natural I should be upset. How could I help it?

When I woke up I found I had gone through something worse than a fainting fit. The excitement had brought on my fever again, and for many days I had been in a very bad way. Mother's face was the first thing before me as I opened my eyes. Father stood close beside her. How they brightened up when they saw that I recognized them! I was greatly surprised to find myself in my own room at home, for I had no idea that we had left the yacht and been on shore nearly two weeks. I had to work hard to collect my thoughts, and even when I remembered that awful scene on the Sound I could not account for my being so feeble and dizzy. Mamma took me in her arms and papa stroked my head, but nothing was said until I managed to whisper my little sister's name. Without speaking, papa turned around and lifted our Daisy out of an arm-chair, where she had been lying asleep. I can't tell you what I felt at the sight
17

of that darling child all safe and well.   But soon
my mind took another turn, and everything grew
mournful and miserable as I thought of the
brave life that had been lost in saving hers.
Papa and mamma must have seen the change in
me, for they looked anxious and perplexed.

"My dear, dear Scar," I whispered again.   I
could not myself hear the words distinctly, but
the moment they passed my lips there was a
rustle on the carpet at the foot of the bed, and
instantly after I felt something moist and comfortable and familiar touching my hand.   Weak
as I was, I pulled myself up on the pillow, and
—oh! joyful sight!—there was Scar, bouncing up
and down, thumping the floor in his lovely, awkward style, and giving me his word as a dog of
honor that he had never in his life been so happy as he was that moment.   He couldn't have
been happier than I, bless him! though he had
the advantage of me in being able to make more
noise about it.

It was Uncle Richard I had to thank for res-
cuing Scar.   While all was in confusion on
board the yacht, Uncle Richard saw what had
occurred, and without stopping even to take off
his spectacles, he jumped into the water, caught
the dog, and held him up until the watchman
who couldn't swim went out in the boat once

more. On this occasion he was made to understand that he mustn't leave anybody behind. Uncle Richard always was my favorite, and if he didn't know it before, he knew it the next time he came to see me.

"It's all right, Arty," he said. "Battered old veterans like Scar and myself are bound to help one another. He would like nothing better than to do me an equally good turn in his own fashion."

It was Uncle Richard, too, who gave Scar the medal that hangs from his collar. It is a small copy of the medal which Congress gave my uncle for gallantry during the war. When a dog can wear such a decoration as that, and has the respect of a Union brigadier-general, and the love and gratitude of a family like ours, he need not be envious of other dogs' beauty. That's what I say, and so says Scar.

TRY AGAIN TRESCOTT'S WAGER

A Fourth of July Adventure

I

Iᴛ is the meanest thing that ever was done!"
exclaimed an excited youngster about ten years
old, who stood surrounded by a disconsolate
group in the playground of Mr Brace's school.

"So it is!" cried another, in still greater agitation. "Nobody but Jim Potter would play such
a trick."

"What shall we do?" demanded a third.
"Can't we get somebody to help us?"

No one was ready with a reply, and the lads
looked ruefully at one another in silence, until
their attention was attracted by the approach of
an older boy, who came running down the steps
of the school-house, in which he had been detained later than the others.

"Here's Try Again Trescott," shouted the little complainant who had first spoken. "Let us tell him about it."

"He'll only laugh at us," said the youngest of the party.

"Who cares for that? He doesn't like Jim Potter, and I know he will do something. You see if he won't. I say, wait a minute, Try Again Trescott!"

Charles Trescott was his proper name, but all his comrades, and, in fact, everybody who knew him, called him Try Again Trescott, in consequence of a peculiar habit which distinguished him among the juvenile populace of New Milford, where he was attending school during the summer. He did not belong to that pleasant Connecticut village, but had been sent thither from New York to live and study during the absence of his parents in Europe. Most of his associates thought him a good sort of fellow, though in the early days of his residence he was held in rather low esteem on account of his complete ignorance of the rural sports and pastimes in which the young people of that region chiefly delighted. He could neither fish nor swim, knew nothing of the management of a boat, and had never mounted a horse in his life. The diversions of woods and fields and hills were all strange to him. Of the higher enjoyments of streams and lakes he was

wholly incapable. For a time it really did seem
that he was not good for much of anything
which country boys care for.

But this lasted only a little while. Those who
made fun of his awkwardness, and jeered at his
efforts to become familiar with out-door exercises,
presently found that he had resolved to partici-
pate sooner or later in every one of the local
amusements. He was not very quick to learn,
but his perseverance and determination carried
him through difficulties which nobody imagined
he could conquer alone. Whenever he failed in
any trial—and he failed a great many times—he
took his discomfiture good-naturedly, and simply
said he would "try again." His first attempt to
keep himself afloat in the Housatonic River was
a dismal exhibition. He went to the bottom like
a lump of lead, and swallowed so much water
that he declared he did not expect to be thirsty
again for a month. But he "tried again," morning and evening, practising all alone in the little
Mystic, a shallow branch of the Housatonic, and
long before the other boys supposed he had
learned enough to keep his head above the
waves, he plunged in among them one day, and
astonished them by offering to race with Jim
Potter. who was the youthful champion of the
town in more than one line of achievement.

Trescott was beaten badly, and everybody jeered at his audacity in matching himself against so redoubtable an opponent. He acknowledged the defeat becomingly, but intimated that it would do no harm to try again; and a fortnight later he had the satisfaction of distancing Jim Potter by three lengths, in a turn around the half-sunken log which marked the usual swimming course.

By carrying the same methods into his studies, he won the good-will of his teacher and a high place in his class, although he never seemed to accomplish any particular thing with especial skill or startling brilliancy. His schoolmates could not understand how he managed to rise above most of them, when it was evident that half a dozen or more were at least quite as clever as he. Jim Potter said, contemptuously, that Trescott had "a sneaking way of getting ahead." But Jim Potter was far from popular, and his bad opinion was not generally shared, notwithstanding that he tried in every way he could think of to create an ill-feeling against the city boy. Very few could be brought to believe there was anything "sneaking" in Charley Trescott's way of gradually mastering Potter at his own games. Even at marbles, in which the village leader's expertness was held to be almost super-

human, the new-comer acquired such prowess
that he became the possessor of the entire magnificent collection which his rival had previously
won from less dexterous players. Trescott would
not keep them, however. He gave the whole lot
back, saying that he could get all the marbles
he wanted without gambling; and that somebody had told him gambling was poor business
for a boy to take hold of. Then Jim Potter
scoffed at Trescott worse than ever, and proclaimed his conviction that such a prig ought to
be roundly dealt with for setting himself up as a
censor of the juvenile society of New Milford.

It was certain that Potter's notions with regard to gambling were not at all disturbed by
his competitor's criticism, for he continued the
practice with the same diligence as before, and
with even greater success. Having won all the
available marbles of the community, he went on
persuading his victims to stake other articles of
property, and in the course of time contrived to
accumulate a veritable museum of fish-hooks,
jack-knives, loadstones, burning-glasses, and similar treasures. Most of these spoils had been
gathered in from boys much younger than himself, who, having an accurate knowledge of Potter's superior strength and lively temper, did not
venture to make open protest, and had to con-

tent themselves with looking glum and exchanging doleful confidences.

But within the past fortnight Potter had proceeded to extremities which roused the most timid to rebellion.   Fourth of July was near at hand, and the young folks had been busily collecting materials for an appropriate celebration. Everybody had at least something ready with which to make patriotic noises and blazes on the glorious anniversary, and a few fortunate individuals were so liberally provided as to excite very unwholesome feelings of envy in the minds of their less-favored companions.   Then it was that Jim Potter began to propose playing marbles for choice fireworks, craftily offering odds, which he pretended would equalize the chances between himself and those whose fingers were not so nimble as his own.   The result was that two days before the jubilee he had become almost the sole possessor of the splendid assortment of crackers, pin-wheels, Roman candles, rockets, blue-lights, and the like, which had previously been distributed widely among the youthful inhabitants of the town.

This was not all, though it was hard enough, and perhaps the worst to bear. A travelling show-man had come to the village on the 1st of July with a sleight-of-hand exhibition, to which

he offered admission at a very low price to all
the boys of Mr. Brace's school. Many had availed
themselves of this privilege ; but that greedy Jim
Potter had actually managed, by his usual methods, to get hold of the greater number of the
tickets, which he straightway disposed of to a
body of his personal followers. This select party
had attended the first performance on the evening of the 2d, and through the greater part of
the following day had been so wildly extrava-
gant in expressing admiration that the poor little
fellows who had foolishly thrown away their
chances were driven into a frenzy of irritation
and disappointment. It was to discuss their woes,
and, if possible, to devise means of redress, that
the small committee had assembled in the manner set forth at the beginning of this story.

II

TRY AGAIN TRESCOTT listened to their lamenta-
tions, and was sorry for them, yet he did not see
his way clear to doing anything for their relief.
He had, stored away at home, a first-class lot of
fireworks — finer, indeed, than that which Jim
Potter had accumulated by his knavish tricks—

which had been sent him as a present by an uncle in New York. Possibly the unhappy sufferers thought he would generously offer to share with them some portion of his rich abundance. The impulse to do so was not wanting, but it was hard for him, as it would have been hard for any boy, to make up his mind to such a sacrifice at such a time. It was not only these half-dozen who had been fleeced, but pretty nearly the whole school, and if he once began giving away, there was no telling where he could stop. While he was rapidly considering the matter, loud voices were heard in the street, and a minute after, Jim Potter, the originator of the trouble, came prancing in with two or three of his chums, chattering eagerly about the wonderful feats they had witnessed the night before.

"Try Again Trescott thinks he knows everything," cried Potter, "because he comes from New York, but I bet he never saw such a show as this."

"I wouldn't care to see it in the way you did," answered Trescott, quietly.

"The man put an apple on another man's hand," continued Potter, paying no attention to Trescott's remark, "and took a big, sharp, heavy sword, and swung it round in the air, and cut right through the apple, whiz!—cut it in halves

—without touching the other fellow's hand. Makes your eyes wink to think of it."

"Was he frightened?" asked one of the small lads, quite carried away by the glowing description.

"Who? The other fellow? I guess not! The man offered to do it to any of us. Looked straight at me, too."

"Did you try it?" demanded the little questioner, breathlessly.

"Try it?" echoed Potter, scornfully. "What are you talking about?"

"Why not?" said Trescott.

"Oh yes. Why not? Think I want to have my hand cut off?"

"He wouldn't ask you," Trescott replied, "if he wasn't sure he could do it without hurting you."

"Get out! Do you mean to say *you* would let him?"

"I don't know; perhaps I would."

"Bet you a set of jack-stones you wouldn't!" exclaimed Potter, whose thoughts were always running on his favorite occupation.

"I don't bet very often, Jim Potter, but I don't believe there was anything to be scared at."

"Oh, of course, you know all about it. I suppose you think you could do the trick yourself."

"I suppose anybody could do it if he learned how."

"Bet you a pickled lime you couldn't."

Trescott did not seem disposed to continue the conversation, but Potter had no notion of letting it drop.

"Bet you a box of fire-crackers you couldn't," he persisted.

Trescott made no response.

"Bet you two boxes of fire-crackers and six Roman candles you can't knock an apple off my hand with a stick that way, and not touch me."

Again Trescott was silent.

"Bet you half my lot of fireworks against half of yours."

The younger boys had listened without uttering a word up to this point, but now one of them broke in:

"Oh, do it, Try Again Trescott," he cried; "do it, and give us the fireworks. You won't want them; you have enough."

Trescott smiled, and shook his head.

"Bet you the whole of my fireworks against yours," shouted Potter, his face red with fierce excitement.

Raising his head, Trescott looked the plunderer squarely in the eyes for a moment, and then said, slowly, "I'll take that bet, Jim Potter."

"'I'LL TAKE THAT BET, JIM POTTER'"

His manner was so serious and earnest that, while the little lads cheered and screamed tumultuously, Potter drew back a step as if in doubt as to the wisdom of his proposal. But he soon rallied, and began to name his conditions.

"No fooling with swords," he said; "I won't stand that. You've got to take a stick and swing it round with all your might, and knock an apple off my right hand without touching me. I'll find the apple."

" Yes," replied Trescott, "and you'll see that it's a small one. I'll find the stick, and I'll see that it's a big one."

" That won't do you any good," sneered Potter, putting on a bold face, though he was more than a little daunted by his opponent's confidence. " But, hold on; you've never tried this trick?"

" I never heard of it in my life."

" All right, then; you bring your fireworks, and I'll bring mine. We'll settle it any time you like."

" To-morrow morning, then," said Trescott, " at eight o'clock, here in this playground."

III

THE news of the wager and the expected contest flew around like the flash of a catherine-wheel. Trescott's consent to take part in one of Potter's questionable games was a surprise to the New Milford boys, for his reluctance to engage in anything that looked like gambling was well known. It was observed, however, that he called

on the evening of the 3d at the house of his
teacher, kind old Mr. Brace, remaining there
about half an hour, and that when he came out
he was in the liveliest spirits and the best of
humors. Was it possible that he had told Mr.
Brace the whole story, and obtained his sanc-
tion to the proceedings? This, however, was put
aside as a minor consideration. The interest and
curiosity of the youthful community were fixed
exclusively upon the coming event.

At eight o'clock on the morning of the Fourth
a great crowd was collected in the playground.
Trescott was one of the first to arrive with a
bundle, or, rather, a set of bundles, so large that
it seemed impossible for Potter to produce a display of equal value. It was indeed evident when
he came upon the scene that his ill-gotten store
was not to be compared with that of his antagonist, and some of the boys pointed this out, sug-
gesting that the stakes were not fairly propor-
tioned. But Potter insisted that the terms of
the bet had been plainly understood, and that
each combatant was to risk the total amount of
his combustible possessions.

"All right," said Trescott. "He shall have it
his own way. Let us get through with it as
soon as we can."

"I suppose you have been practising all night

long," grumbled Potter, with a sniff of affected disdain.

"I never took the stick in my hand till half an hour ago," Trescott said to his own friends, rather than in response to his adversary.

"Bet you ten fish-hooks you did!" cried Potter, who lost no chance of repeating his invariable proposition.

The preparations were promptly made. Potter produced from his pocket the tiniest of crab-apples, at which there was a shout of derision.

"It's an apple, anyway," asserted the village gambler. "I have a right to choose my own kind."

"Let him do as he likes; a small apple suits me best," said Trescott, to everybody's amazement, and somewhat to the consternation of Potter and his party, all of whom were startled, and their leader especially, by this cool and un-looked-for announcement.

But there was no possibility of stopping the affair at this point. Potter stretched out his hand, and the withered little crab-apple was deposited on the palm. The New York lad flourished his weapon in the air. It was a stout walking-stick, with a big curved handle, and the staring spectators noticed, with considerable wonder, that Trescott held it by the ferrule end.

18

Thrice he whirled it around his head, and then the stroke was given. Was the apple touched? Not by the cane, at any rate. The heavy handle crashed against Jim Potter's knuckles with a thwack that might have been heard at each extremity of the village, and been mistaken for the report of a giant torpedo. The apple dropped to the ground, while he who held it danced and howled and blew upon his fingers in a frenzy of pain and rage. The greater number of the witnesses were delighted with the result of the experiment so far as its immediate effect upon Potter was concerned, and the little boys threw themselves down and rolled about in ecstasies. For the moment they thought only of the punishment of their persecutor, and gave no heed to after consequences.

A minute passed before the sufferer could control his voice and speak coherently. Then he marched up to Trescott and shook his injured fist at him.

"I'll pay you for this some day," he screamed; "but, first of all, I'll take those fine fireworks of yours. They belong to me now."

The sounds of acclamation suddenly ceased. The transitory joy awakened by the spectacle of the public enemy's anguish gave way to a deep despondency. At the thought that their last

"THE NEW YORK LAD FLOURISHED HIS WEAPON IN THE AIR"

hope of restitution was gone, the youngsters wailed aloud. In the midst of general confusion, Potter, with two or three followers, advanced to seize the coveted prizes; but as they were about to lay hands on them, they were checked by Trescott, who sprang forward, brandishing his cane with an air of defiance, before which the spoilers instinctively fell back.

"Wait, there, Jim Potter!" he called out, in ringing tones. "I haven't finished yet. I've only just begun. I never said I could do it the first time. You know my name. I'm Try Again Trescott!"

The boys stood motionless, gazing in stupefaction at one another, until the full meaning of the situation burst upon them. When the conviction spread that Potter had been foiled and outwitted, a cry of exultation arose the like of which had seldom been heard in New Milford on any Fourth of July since the nation was born. For a brief instant the baffled depredator thought of attempting to secure by force the booty which had escaped from his clutch, but a glance showed him that the boys were in no temper to be further trifled with, and he turned upon Trescott with malignant spite.

"Keep your fireworks, you cheat!" he yelled. "Give me my lot, if you don't mean to steal them."

" I'm not a cheat nor a thief," replied Trescott. " You all know me pretty well. I always have to try more than once before I can do anything I undertake. Hold out your apple, Jim Potter."

In his bewilderment the fellow did actually pick up the apple and balance it on his hand as before; but when he saw the dreadful stick descending his small stock of pluck vanished, and he jerked his arm away with such alacrity that the whole crowd hooted at him. After this it would have been useless to bluster. He looked around just once, with a black and scowling face, and then stole away, not a single one of even his own set accompanying him. It was a short and easy job to redistribute the recovered fireworks among the original owners. A few had been used on the previous evening, but these were made good by Trescott from his own ample supply, with a cheerfulness that made him, at least for the time, the most popular boy in that region. Independence Day ran through its course with more than common merriment, and it was long before the lads of New Milford ceased to remember their debt of gratitude to the quick wit and ready resolution of Try Again Trescott.

A FRIEND IN NEED

I

N a bright autumn afternoon in the year 1863, a pleasant-faced and dark-complexioned young gentleman was walking rapidly through the principal avenue of a small city in western New York. He was hurrying to catch a railway train, but as he passed the open door of a public hall he saw something which caused him to stop abruptly. A pretty child, apparently about eight years old, was standing at the entrance looking anxiously up and down the street, and silently crying.

"What is the matter, little one?" asked the gentleman, going up the steps towards her.

She turned her tearful eyes upon him, and made an effort to control her grief.

"Bessie doesn't come," she answered, in a trembling voice.

"That is too bad," said the stranger. "Is Bessie ill?"

"I don't know; she doesn't come, and we're 'fraid the concert will be spoiled."

"But you mustn't spoil your rosy cheeks for that, my dear. Are you all alone?" He spoke with a slight foreign accent, but in so gentle and kindly a tone that the child's good-will was immediately won. She was about to reply, when two or three older girls came out from the hall, and by involuntary exclamations expressed their surprise at finding her in conversation with an unknown person.

"Excuse me," he said, nodding his head and smiling. "I am trying to console this little lady. I can't bear to see young people cry."

"It is about Bessie," explained the oldest of the children, whose age might have been eleven or twelve. "She has disappointed us terribly."

"Can you tell me about it?" inquired the gentleman, putting on an appearace of great interest. In fact, he *was* interested. His fondness for little folks was well known to many persons and in many places, and he never seemed better contented than in their company.

"We are going to give a concert," said the leader of the party, after a moment's hesitation, "for the Sanitary Commission. At least, we *were* going to. But we can't do without Bessie, and this is our last rehearsal."

"Perhaps she is sick. Can't you rehearse again?"

"Oh no; the concert is for to-night. Bessie plays the second part in the overture and all the other piano pieces."

"May I ask what the overture is?"

"The 'Crown Diamonds.' It's *very* difficult. Four of us play it on two pianos."

"I understand. Let us step into the vestibule; perhaps I may suggest something. I like music very much."

They all went in, out of sight of persons passing by. The girls were deeply absorbed in their trouble, and gave no thought to the circumstance that they were admitting to their confidence an individual whom none of them had ever before seen.

"What else have you on your programme?" he asked.

"The Pesther Waltzes, and a selection from 'Trovatore,' and the 'Wedding March.' That's the hardest of all."

" And who are the performers ?"

" I play the first part, Bessie Thornton the second, Charlie Jackson the third, and Winnie Jackson here the fourth."

" I'm going to *try*, Florence," said the one who was indicated as Winnie Jackson, with becoming modesty.

" Then Charlie is to play a piece by himself. He's practising it now inside."

" And I shall speak ' 'Celsior,' sha'n't I, Florence ?" interposed the little creature whose grief had first attracted the stranger's notice. She had dried her eyes, and was wholly taken up with the new-comer.

" Yes, Jennie dear — ' *Excelsior*,' " responded Florence. " You see, sir, we have been at work for three weeks. We all belong to the same school, and it's entirely our own idea. Mr. Bush lets us have the hall for nothing, and we hope to make ever so much money—twenty-five dollars, I guess. The tickets are a quarter of a dollar, and all our friends have promised to attend. But, oh dear! what am I saying? If Bessie doesn't come everything will go wrong."

The incident I am relating took place during the heat of the great Civil War, when people of every age all over the Northern States were doing their utmost to lessen the hardships of the

Union soldiers. The Sanitary Commission was a favorite object of charity, and scarcely a day passed without the announcement of some public entertainment, large or small, by professional or amateur performers for the benefit of this important organization.

While the band of youthful patriots stood lamenting the danger that threatened their project, a lad of ten years came running in from the sidewalk.

"It's no use, girls," he cried. "Bessie has an awful cold and fever, and her mother won't let her stir out. I don't believe she'll be able to come this evening, either."

A wail of despair broke from the despondent group.

"But there's a *chance* that she can join you to-night," said the sympathizing gentleman.

"That wouldn't do us any good," moaned Mistress Florence. "We shouldn't dare to play without another rehearsal, and we can't rehearse without Bessie."

"Why not?" urged the friend in need. "Come, I see that I have lost my train. I will take Bessie's part for you this afternoon, at any rate."

"Can you?" exclaimed Florence, much astonished at this unexpected proposition.

"Why, certainly; I have nothing to do."

"But—I mean—" The little girl became embarrassed, and could not end the sentence.

"She means," said Winnie Jackson, coming to her companion's aid—"she means—please excuse us, but Bessie is a very fine player; the best we have, next to Florence."

"Oh, well, give me a trial," replied the stranger, laughing. "I used to play pretty well when I was your age."

"I'm sorry if I was rude; pray forgive me," Florence begged. "It will be *so* kind if you can —if you *will* help us."

"Of course I will."

"Hooray! I call that splendid!" shouted the youngster who had brought the bad tidings from Bessie Thornton's house. "Just come out here, Charlie; a gentleman has volunteered to take Bessie's place at rehearsal. Will you tell me your name, sir?"

"You may call me Mr. Moreau."

A few minutes later Mr. Moreau was seated at Florence's left side, dutifully sustaining his part in an eight-hand arrangement of Auber's lively overture. When this had been gone through twice, the tiny maid Jennie, who had watched the performance with critical solemnity, delivered her mind to the new member of the quartet thus:

"A FEW MINUTES LATER MR. MOREAU WAS SEATED AT
FLORENCE'S LEFT SIDE"

"Very nice. You do play 'most as well as Bessie. Doesn't he, Flo?"

"He plays better, dear," answered Florence. "I think," she added, timidly, "that he isn't doing all he can. I'm not sure, but it seems as if he must know more than any of us."

"'Cept you, Flo," said the small judge, with decisive emphasis.

The other pieces were then taken up, and one or two passages which puzzled Florence's fingers in the "Wedding March" were modified by Mr. Moreau so adroitly that she was able, after following his advice, to give all the required effect without getting the notes confused or disturbing the time.

When the rehearsal was about half over, the inner door of the hall leading from the vestibule was softly pushed open, and a lady entered, so quietly that her presence was not remarked by the busy pianists. She took a few steps towards the stage, stopped suddenly on perceiving the addition to the expected number of its occupants, and stood as if overpowered by amazement. After gazing intently for some seconds, she cautiously withdrew and went into the street, with a peculiar expression of wonderment upon her countenance.

Mr. Moreau not only acted as Bessie's substi-

tute in the instrumental music, but undertook
also the accompaniment to a song that Florence
was to sing. He complimented her upon the
freshness and sweetness of her voice, and the
good taste with which she used it.

"Ah, Mr. Moreau," she said, simply and earnestly, "I never sang it so well before. Almost
always I am frightened, but your beautiful accompaniment makes me feel perfectly safe and
sure."

"Thank you, Miss Florence," he replied. "People are not often praised so honestly and sincere-
ly as that."

"I can't say how much we are obliged to you,"
she continued. "If Bessie will only come to-
night we can get through, after all."

"And if she does not?"

"Oh, it makes me miserable to think of
such a thing! All our trouble will go for
nothing."

"And I can't speak ''Celsior,'" piped Jennie,
disconsolately.

"Now, listen to me, my little friends; I am
not going to do my work by halves. I will stay
in town and come here myself, and if your invalid does not appear, you shall have my services
and welcome."

There was a loud outcry of enthusiasm and

delight, and happier faces never were seen than those which were gratefully upturned to the good-natured unknown.

Just as they were about to separate, the superintendent of the hall, Mr. Bush, came along. He gave a queer start on seeing Mr. Moreau, and would have called out to him if he had not been checked by a hasty signal from that gentleman. He waited without speaking until the children had gone, and then said,

"I thought you were on your way to New York?"

"So I am," answered Mr. Moreau. "I left by the three o'clock train. Don't contradict me, and don't allow anybody to make the mistake of supposing that I am here."

"Just as you like," returned Mr. Bush, chuckling. "No one shall hear a word from me."

II

FLORENCE LYNWOOD ran home with her sister in high spirits, eager to relate what had happened, and anxious to secure her mother's approval of the plan to be adopted in case of Bessie Thornton's continued illness.

"Mamma," she cried, "I have something ever so strange to tell you."

"I know a part of it," said Mrs. Lynwood. "I looked in at the hall this afternoon."

"Then you saw the strange gentleman?"

"Yes, for a moment. Did he tell you his name?"

"His name is Morrow," chirped little Jennie, who wished it to be understood that she also had information to impart.

"Morrow," repeated Mrs. Lynwood. "That is singular."

"It sounded like that," said Florence. "I think he is a foreigner." She went on to describe him as well as she could, and to give the particulars of his friendly behavior. "And, mamma," she concluded, "if Bessie stays at home this evening, he is going to play her part in all the piano pieces."

"Really!" exclaimed her mother, showing much more interest than Florence had expected. "From what I hear, Bessie certainly cannot venture out. You are sure this gentleman will not disappoint you?"

"Oh, mamma, he is too kind for that."

"I hope so. Now, my daughter, you shall hear some good news. You have reckoned upon getting twenty-five dollars for the Sanitary Commission. Well, your concert shall bring you at least a hundred if you will get together as many schoolmates as you can find in half an hour, and bring them here without delay. Don't ask me to explain; I want to write as rapidly as possible. Lose no time, my dear, and come back in thirty minutes."

Florence was in ecstasy at the brilliant prospect held out to her, and started on her errand without a word of inquiry. When she returned, accompanied by ten or twelve juvenile acquaintances, her mother was ready with a score of notes, which she now addressed and handed to the children, to be delivered to their parents and neighbors. These epistles were all alike in substance. They briefly stated a certain fact, and requested that the intelligence should be promptly and extensively distributed. Within the following hour the circle of society in which Mrs. Lynwood moved was glowing with an excitement the like of which had seldom been witnessed in that quiet interior city.

III

At eight o'clock in the evening the hall was
crowded with the largest and most distinguished
audience ever gathered within its walls.   Mr.
Moreau arrived in good season, and made his
way by a private passage to the room reserved
for the performers, just as a final message from
Bessie Thornton's parents was received, expressing regret at the sick girl's positive inability to
join in the proceedings.

"Oh, Mr. Moreau," said Florence, "what should
we have done without you, and how shall I thank
you for your goodness?"

"How?   Easily enough, my dear child.   By
singing your pretty song as well this evening as
you did this afternoon."

Precisely at the appointed hour Master Jackson led his sister to her place at the piano and
seated himself beside her.   They were warmly
welcomed; but when Mr. Moreau appeared with
Florence Lynwood's hand in his, the applause
was so overwhelming that the young girl was
startled.   She was quick enough to guess, however, that there must be some stronger cause for

Valentine Adams

"MASTER JACKSON LED HIS SISTER TO HER PLACE"

the extraordinary demonstration than the mere entrance of two or three school children. She glanced shyly at her escort, but could see nothing in his face that helped to throw light on the situation.

The concert was a prodigious success from beginning to end. The programme was not very long, and was all over at an early hour, notwithstanding that everything was encored, including Jennie's recitation of "Excelsior," and Florence was recalled three times after her song. Just before the last number was performed, Mr. Bush marched upon the stage and made a bit of a speech. He said he was deputed by the ladies and gentlemen present to declare their gratification at meeting under such agreeable and novel circumstances the eminent artist to whom they had been so often indebted for the highest enjoyment, and to express the hope that he would favor them at the close of the entertainment with an exhibition of his own rare skill and power. Since he had done so much for the youth of the community, he trusted it would not be presumptuous for the grown-up citizens to ask a boon on their own behalf.

Mr. Moreau, who had been listening at the side of the stage, now came forward, and was again saluted with fervor. As soon as he could be heard he gracefully acknowledged the greeting bestowed upon him, and frankly avowed the pleasure it had given him to co-operate in the worthy entertainment of his young associates.

"It was my fortune to be born at the South," he said, "but no man can be more devoted to the Union than I, or more ready to contribute his share in relieving the suffering of our sick and wounded soldiers. When I can do it in such company as this"—and he waved his hand towards the children—" I feel a happiness far different from that which the commonplace successes of life produce, and which I truly do not know how to describe. My accidental participation in this event will be one of my most charming recollections. As to the request which you have made through Mr. Bush, I should consider it an honor to comply without any conditions, if I were free to follow my own inclination. But I am here to support the exertions of my young friends on behalf of a noble object, and I am bound on this occasion to do nothing that shall not add to the good result of their endeavor. They have invited you to an excellent concert, and you have responded liberally. So far the account is even. I must see that it continues so to the end. I shall gladly play for you, but we will, if you please, introduce my music with a good old-fashioned ceremony. We will take up a special contribution to the Sanitary Commission. If you will allow me, I will go through the aisle at the right, and I shall ask my fellow - artist, Miss Lynwood, to look after the left. Here, Miss Florence, take Mr. Bush's hat, and let me have the privilege of making the first deposit."

He suited the action to the word, and drawing from his pocket a coin rarely seen in those days of paper currency — a twenty-dollar gold piece, worth not less than forty or fifty dollars of the money in common use—he held it up to view, probably as a stimulating example to the spectators, and dropped it into the superintendent's hat, which he then handed to Florence, and sent her on the round of collection. Bringing his own hat from the anteroom, he started at the opposite side of the hall, laughing and chatting merrily as he passed along the rows of seats. "I am getting on famously," he cried at one point; "let us see which of us will take the larger sum. Surely you will not be less generous to one of your own daughters than to a visitor from afar." Soon after he said, "I shall be astonished if you do not make my hat heavier than the young lady's; this city has a reputation for hospitality to sustain, and you will not be so selfish as to let a guest fall behind one of your own citizens." The audience, though taken by surprise, was greatly diverted, and not at all slow in partaking of his merry humor. There was no stinginess for him to complain of. When he returned to the stage he carried with him a fraction over one hundred dollars. He would not begin playing till the amount was counted and reported. Florence was even more successful. She brought up close upon one hundred and twenty dollars. Then it was that she had that lucky inspiration which gained her the name of being the brightest and quickest girl of her age in town.

"We are just alike," she said. And as he made a sign of dissent, she insisted: "Oh yes, we are. You had no right to put twenty dollars in my hat and nothing in yours. I shall divide your gift, and call it ten dollars for me and ten for you. Then we shall each have one hundred and ten."

This was the great hit of the evening so far. But the music that followed caused everything else to be forgotten, at least for the time. The pianist kept on with unflagging amiability and spirit for more than half an hour, and when he rose, at eleven o'clock, the people were hoarse from shouting his name. The children could not make out the word that everybody was crying, and Florence, bending over from the platform, asked her mother what it was.

"Is it possible you do not know, my dear?" exclaimed Mrs. Lynwood. "It is the name of the greatest of American pianists."

"Oh, *now* I understand! But you told us,"

said Florence, turning to the artist, "that your name was Moreau."

"And so it is, my child," he answered. "I am Louis Moreau Gottschalk." *

APPENDIX

A PATRIOTIC PIANIST

THE most celebrated pianist produced by the United States was a native of New Orleans named Gottschalk, who died, while still quite young, about twenty-five years ago. He was of French descent, and as French was the language of his childhood, he spoke English with an accent which often caused strangers to mistake him for a foreigner. But he was as thorough an American as ever breathed, and was conspicuously faithful to his country at a time when most men of Southern birth acknowledged no obligation of loyalty, and sought to destroy the great republic by establishing a separate nation for themselves.

His life, like that of many distinguished musi-

---

* See Appendix—" A Patriotic Pianist."

cians, was passed chiefly in travelling about the world and giving concerts. His popularity was remarkable, not only on account of his artistic gifts, but also because of his varied personal attractions. The charm of his manner and his refined courtesy won him hosts of friends in every place which he visited. But with all his gentleness of demeanor, he had an abundance of manly spirit and courage, as those who presumed upon his natural amiability were sure to learn.

In 1862, when the war of secession was at its height, his public engagements carried him to Canada, where he was less known than in his own land. His first appearance was in a large city, the inhabitants of which had been informed that he came from New Orleans, but were wholly unaware of his strong feeling against slavery or his earnest devotion to the Union. Our Canadian neighbors were not, as a rule, well disposed to the Northern cause. Their sympathy was with the States in revolt, and they were not backward in proclaiming the fact. The advent of the famous young Southerner seemed to afford them an unusually fine opportunity of avowing their sentiments. Taking it for granted, without inquiry, that he stood with the people of his State and "section," they made up their minds to pay him what they considered a very pretty compliment, and at the same time to indulge themselves with a lively demonstration of their fondness for the Confederacy.

The concert was attended by an immense audience, and Gottschalk was greeted with an ardor which somewhat surprised him. He had no suspicion that he was regarded as a representative of the rebellion, and it was not until the end of the evening that anything occurred to enlighten him. As he came forward for the last time, a loud call for "Dixie" went up from the multitude. He looked about in amazement, not understanding at first the meaning of the cry. While he stood irresolute, the demand was loudly repeated, and followed by a wild chorus of acclamation for secessionists in general. Presently a diversion was made in favor of "My Maryland," one party clamoring for that stately air, while another continued to shout for the more hilarious ditty.

It was a trying position for the pianist. He believed that a refusal would give intense irritation at the moment, and would probably endanger his entire expedition through the British province. The wayward public is prodigal of bounty and caresses so long as its caprices are humored, but at the least sign of opposition, it is liable to turn upon its idols and rend them.

It was no trifling undertaking for one man to defy the will of this excited throng. Yet his resolve was taken without an instant's hesitation. Though he felt that by his own act he would bring his tour to an ignominious end, he saw but one course open to him. He waited until the uproar subsided, and bowing ceremoniously, seated himself at his instrument. For a brief interval all was silence; then his hands fell upon the keys; but neither "Dixie" nor "My Maryland" came in response to his touch. "Hail Columbia" was the strain that resounded through the hall and fell upon the ears of the astonished Canadians.

The tumult that immediately ensued deadened the sound of the music, and the performer desisted from his labor. Imagining that he was terrified into submission, the audience signified a willingness to give him another chance. There was a lull in the storm, and Gottschalk, after bowing as formally as before, turned once more to his task. This time he chose "Yankee Doodle," which was no sooner recognized than a fresh outburst of disapprobation made his efforts again inaudible.

"It did not matter to me," he said, relating the story afterwards. "I was determined to stay there all night if necessary—unless I was dragged from the platform—and give them an unmistakable Union melody as often as I could get a hearing. The only thing that worried me was that we had no national song worthy of the name. I could not use 'The Star-spangled Banner,' which is a capital tune, because the music is not American. But though my material was not first-class, I tried to make up for that by good playing. After a while the people grew tired of raging at me, and then they heard me at my best—my very best, I assure you."

"And how did it end?" the pianist was asked.

"Oh, very unexpectedly, and most happily. They had kept ominously still a long time, and I was wondering what mischief was in store, when a man with a big heavy voice suddenly broke out laughing. That settled everything. In less than a minute the whole audience was laughing, too, in the pleasantest possible humor. They began to cheer me as if I had done nothing but what they wanted, and I suppose my independence made them think better of me than if I had yielded. From that night I was treated in the most friendly way. While I remained in Canada there was no indication that I had given offence by my obstinacy, and pretty soon I found that I was expected to introduce some specimens of genuine Yankee minstrelsy at every concert,

whether the programme promised them or not.
I never objected to this, of course; but it made
me wretched that the country I belonged to had
no other rallying songs than a few bits of cheap
jig music. If I live long enough, I must try my
own hand at producing a ' national anthem.' "

He did not live long enough; and it is strange
to reflect that this brilliant artist, who from the
age of fourteen until his early death enjoyed a
renown beyond that of any other American vir-
tuoso, is now almost forgotten by the public. A
quarter of a century ago he was unrivalled in
his vocation, and the first of social favorites.
Wherever he went he endeared himself alike to
old and young, yet the rising generation of to-
day scarcely knows his name. But his rare and
beautiful compositions will long be cherished by
musicians. They have the glow of true genius,
and works thus inspired possess a lasting claim
to respectful remembrance.

THE END.

www.ingramcontent.com/pod-product-compliance
Lightning Source LLC
Chambersburg PA
CBHW021117270326
41929CB00009B/927